H.E.N.R.Y. STRATEGIES UNLOCKED

H.E.N.R.Y. STRATEGIES UNLOCKED

How to Build a Plan That Works As Hard As You Do

GIDEON DRUCKER, CFP® AIF® ECA

Redwood Publishing, LLC
Orange County, California

Published by Redwood Publishing, LLC
Orange County, California
www.redwooddigitalpublishing.com

Printed in the United States of America

ISBN 978-1-966333-27-2 (hardcover)
ISBN 978-1-966333-28-9 (paperback)
ISBN 978-1-966333-29-6 (e-book)

Book Design:
    Cover Design: Michelle Manley, Graphique Design Co., LLC
    Interior Design: Creative Publishing Book Design

First Edition

HOW DO YOU
GET THERE ?

↓

WHERE ARE
YOU TODAY ? ―――――――――――――― WHERE DO
YOU WANT
TO GO ?

BEHAVIOR GAP

CONTENTS

Part 4: Hiring an Advisor: Picking the Right One for You

Part 5: Conclusion

FOREWORD

The Chairman (Gideon's Dad)
Gets His Say

Three years ago, Gideon and I were out swimming in the ocean at Montauk. I looked over at him and said, "Congrats, you are now the guy." He figured it was just another dad thing and shot back, "What does that mean?" I told him I was stepping down as President of the firm, and he'd be running the show. I had no idea how seriously he'd take that—and how far he'd run with it.

By sheer will and grit, Gideon took our firm independent. We became a Fiduciary RIA, launched an estate planning division, a tax division, started hiring and training advisors, and saw geometric growth. Somewhere in the middle of all that, he married his kind, beautiful wife.

I started in this business over forty years ago, and I've seen a lot of changes in the financial planning universe—most of them good ones. Technology, index funds, passive investing, the lowering of costs to own "the market," and now AI, with all the mostly good things that come with it. But the one constant? Some folks are going to want to do it all themselves and some see the value of professional guidance. In my experience, to be great at anything—financial planning, Brazilian Jiu Jitsu, you name it—having a Sherpa or a coach to help guide you, to provide expertise and outside perspective and to help you over the bumps, speeds your progress.

Gideon has become a thought leader in our industry, as evidenced by all his top advisor awards that I can't keep track of. He's dedicated to spreading the gospel of financial planning—almost to the point of obsession. Hence, this second book.

Every generation says the next lacks the fire they had. But this book? This was written by a man filled with passion, for like-minded folks who are willing to put in the work to achieve their lifetime financial goals. If you don't appreciate the grind, if you don't have the grit and desire to work hard for the things you want in life, then this book probably isn't for you. For everyone else: read on and buckle up. This will become your roadmap to achieving your financial goals.

— Lance

A NOTE FROM THE AUTHOR
WHY I DO IT

GOALS
&
DREAMS

RESOURCES

YOUR _BEST_ FINANCIAL LIFE

BEHAVIOR GAP

I start every day with a giant cup of coffee, a glass of lemon water (which my wife makes me drink), and a long run along the East River in New York City.

During my run, I listen to one of the ten podcasts in my normal rotation. The podcasts run the gamut: financial planning, business, politics, movies, tennis . . . I listen to them all. Listening to a podcast while running outside is my happy place.

On this morning's run, though, I was barely listening to Andy Roddick recount the miraculous French Open final, in which Carlos Alcaraz somehow defeated Jannik Sinner, because I could not keep my mind from wandering back to the financial plan my team was presenting to two new clients, Marc and Laura, later that day.

The meeting was a big one for them. They had a chance to change the course of their financial future (and to silence that voice in the back of their heads that had them wondering if they were going to be okay)—and I never take that lightly.

I first connected with Marc and Laura three months ago, after Laura attended one of my webinars. As we chatted briefly on an initial "Right Fit" call (a call we use to mutually determine whether we're the right firm for a prospective client), I learned that Marc (forty-five) was a director at a large tech firm and Laura (forty-three) worked in finance. They had an eight-year-old son and a five-year-old daughter, and in their opinion, their finances were all over the place. Now, to be clear, broadly speaking and by any objective measure, they were in the top 0.5% of Americans, with over $600K in annual household income. But wealth is relative, and they felt unorganized and lost, with no plan in place for growing or protecting their wealth. They had a growing concern that their spending and their family's lifestyle were getting out of hand. ("I can't believe how much we spend every month! If you had told us ten years ago we'd be spending like this . . . !" Laura had remarked on our first call.)

They mentioned being too busy with high-demand jobs and family responsibilities (not in that order!) to find the time necessary to allocate their multiple retirement accounts, commit to the "right amount" of insurance, or map out a tax strategy. They lacked estate planning documents or a plan for donating to the organizations important to them. They—understandably—felt overwhelmed. Once we started working together, they passed me the baton and basically said, "Here, please tell us . . . How are we doing?! What are we missing? What do we need to do?"

I don't know how to write this without sounding corny, so here it is: I LIVE FOR THOSE MOMENTS. I really do.

I am obsessed with helping people find their financial footing and take control of their financial future. Getting to serve the role I do for my clients and my growing team of advisors truly gets me out of bed in the morning.

I love being the guy who clients like Marc and Laura turn to for advice and guidance on major life decisions.

I love mapping out long-term scenarios, cash flows, and tactical strategies with clients and then taking decisive action together.

I love establishing the financial foundations that allow our advisors and our clients to be resolute in their financial decision-making.

And most of all . . . I love helping our clients find their financial confidence and peace of mind.

I often think of the Michael Jordan quote that, while he plays more than one hundred games per year, he tries to remember that each night there's some kid watching in the stands who has never seen him play before. (Stay with me. I'm not actually comparing myself to Michael Jordan!)

In a similar vein, Marc and Laura only get to make life-altering financial decisions once. Most likely, this is their only opportunity to talk—out loud—about the intersection of money, family, goals, and priorities. And when it comes to certain financial decisions they're contemplating, there are no do-overs.

Meanwhile, my team and I facilitate these conversations EVERY DAY, and we get to help people like Marc and Laura make the right decisions for their families every week.

My first book—*How to Avoid H. E. N. R. Y. (High Earner Not Rich Yet) Syndrome: Financial Strategies to Own Your Future* (published in 2020)—was all about helping HENRYs.

HENRYs are young professionals who earn great money but are just starting out in their careers (late twenties to mid-thirties). They may not have families (yet) and are just getting introduced to investments, tax planning, and life planning. (To check out that title, visit *The H.E.N.R.Y. Series* on Amazon, where you'll find a purchase link, or scan the QR code below to learn more. You can also find all resources linked throughout this book via the same QR code.)

In this second book, I focus on people exactly like Marc and Laura: mid-career professionals (aged thirty-five to fifty-two) who have the blessing—and dilemma—of making a "dangerously" high income. While still HENRYs, they are usually further along in their careers and family goals and looking for more comprehensive planning and support. If this isn't you yet, don't worry! You'll get there. (In the meantime, you may find my first book helpful!)

But maybe you DO relate to Marc and Laura's story. Maybe you're an attorney, physician, or, like Marc and many of our clients, you're in big tech—you're successful, but with no detailed or coordinated strategy on how to manage your finances. Maybe you're a dual-career couple looking at an upcoming home renovation, baffled as to why your supposedly high income hasn't translated into available cash. Maybe you're raising three kids, and your impressive titles and salaries just aren't adding up to unlock the kind of life you want to live. Or maybe you do EXACTLY what you want day-to-day, but you feel like your FUTURE goals, like retirement, are getting further away. If any of this seems at all relatable . . . well, this was written for you.

This book is meant to serve as an introduction to the financial concepts, stories, and lessons that continue to guide Drucker Wealth and our clients, like Marc and Laura, whom we are fortunate enough to steward. In the following chapters, I'll share my approach to investing, real estate, and tax strategy. I'll offer advice (and stories) to strengthen your financial decision-making process. And ultimately, I'll provide real, tangible tips to guide you on your path toward financial independence.

More than anything, I hope this book moves you to take action in whatever way makes sense for you and your family.

PART 1
FINANCIAL PLANNING AND YOU

"Wealth is the ability to fully experience life."
–Henry David Thoreau

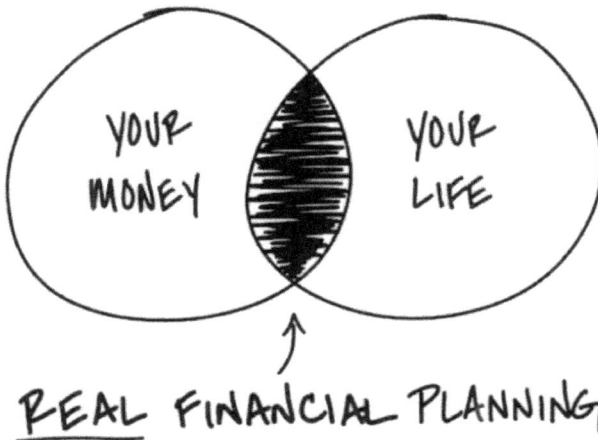

YOUR MONEY

YOUR LIFE

REAL FINANCIAL PLANNING

BEHAVIOR GAP

1

Making a Dangerous
Amount of Money

*"Every financial decision a person makes,
makes sense to them in that moment and
checks the boxes they need to check.
They tell themselves a story about what
they're doing and why they're doing it."*
– Morgan Housel, *The Psychology of Money*

Making a "dangerous" amount of money is a real thing—so real that most of the individuals and families my firm works with use the term regularly as they try to work out this central dichotomy (we'll get there) at the heart of their financial life.

In my experience, a "dangerous" amount of household income is generally $250K to $1M, although I'd say this concept is self-qualifying. You will know immediately if it describes your financial situation because it will seem to perfectly explain the financial decisions (or non-decisions) that you are making day-to-day.

I'll explain it like this: If you're making under $250K and you have a family, you probably have a pretty good handle on how much you're spending, how much you're saving, and what's left over each month—because you need to. Because there's not so much "extra," you have to be diligent about how you're spending your money (even more so if you're committed to any sort of savings goal). That extra $100 dinner out each month? Well, that can go a long way toward building your reserve or paying off debt.

On the flip side, if you're making $3M to $5M a year, you probably don't need to have an automatic savings plan or be super diligent about cash flow. Most likely, and without much thought, you're going to be just fine . . . as long as you're not totally off your rocker in terms of lifestyle! If you're making that much money, you will end up saving enough each year to compound your wealth *and* hit your goals, almost by accident.

But earning mid to high six figures? Your income is high enough for you to be totally comfortable day-to-day—you travel when you want, eat out when you want, can send your kids to camp, hire tennis coaches as often as you want, and money is of no real concern when you think about the next twelve months. In fact, even with relatively lackadaisical spending, you STILL seem to be growing your net worth year-over-year. Your savings account seems to get larger over time (though you have absolutely no idea by how much), you're maxing out your 401(k), and that's usually enough to satisfy your financial concerns. At least for a little bit.

Earning as much as you are, you could just wing it when it comes to planning—and maybe you are. But there's a little voice in the back of your head wondering if that's such a good idea. Because, again, you're not making so much money that you can just sit back and sail into the next phase of life with certitude that you have "enough." In fact, you KNOW—when you really think about it—that financial independence isn't just going to happen.

You still need to allocate money toward specific goals and decide upon the competing priorities at the center of your life—paying for your kids' schools, which includes the price of living in an area that has the best ones; saving for college educations; renovating your home; supporting a spouse or partner through a possible career change; helping your elderly parents; early retirement; buying a vacation home and so on.

Every now and then, the questions hit you: *Are we actually on track? Could we be doing more? Are we going to be okay when the kids' college tuitions come due? Will we be able to retire earlier than our own parents did? Can we even afford a retirement that lives up to our lifestyle?* Over time, and as the voice asking these questions grows louder, you realize you need to take a step back and reassess it all: Are you making intentional financial decisions about your future, or is your income just carrying you from cost to cost?

Because again (and I think it bears repeating), you're past the point of having to worry about every penny that comes in. You can spend as much as you like in your everyday life with no real worries . . . but this can provide a false sense of security. You have this weird, disorienting sense of being totally comfortable in the short term, but you're stressed about the future. This dichotomy can leave you feeling stuck in place, reluctant to plan because it feels overwhelming, and increasingly anxious, because you really don't know where you stand, how much you're going to need, or where your financial blind spots are.

More than anything, making a "dangerous" amount of money is about feeling like you're not living up to your financial potential. It's a feeling that you SHOULD be better off financially than you are, and a fear that if you did step back and look at the big picture, what you'd see would be a lot of unfulfilled potential, and money and years gone to waste. The good news? This is a common financial worry, and I'd argue that it is even more common among those making a "dangerous" amount of money, because of this constant push/pull we're discussing. The even better news? You have ALL the raw materials (high income, compounding assets, and a long-time horizon) necessary to achieve financial independence. You just need a proactive approach to get there!

A lot of these late-night thoughts bubble to the surface when I meet people on introductory calls. Wanting to gauge their current financial health, I ask questions like:

- Do you have a sense of your monthly spending? Is this something you think about a lot?

- How about your saving approach: Do you save a set amount of money each month? Or do you have a process more akin to adding whatever is left over at the end of the month into your savings/investments?

- How do your monthly inflows and outflows usually play out? Do they stress you out, make you feel excited/content, or are they out of sight, out of mind?

The answers can be all over the map, but they usually sound like this:

- "My husband and I make a lot of money; we just feel like we should have more to show for it . . ."

- "My wife and I each have some savings, investments, and retirement accounts . . . but I don't know . . . will it be enough? We have no idea! We need someone to show us."

- "We feel like we're doing a lot of the basic investing and tax stuff, but we don't know what we should be doing next. We feel like there's more we could be doing."
- "We keep making more money each year, but our lifestyle seems to increase just as much. We *need* to do a better job with this. It's time to get organized!"

Fortunately, recognizing an issue and committing yourself to addressing it is half the battle.

After all, when you commit to getting in better physical shape, the acts of showing up at the gym and buying healthier snacks are usually the hardest steps—even though they are the very first steps (and technically you haven't done anything yet). Regardless, it's these initial steps that are the pivot points for the rest of your life.

Similarly, paying heed to that voice in the back of your head that wonders if you're being as intentional with your money as you need to be is a monumental first step.

Learning what to do about it is where we turn next.

2

Financial Priorities vs. Financial Goals

"Money is only a tool. It will take you wherever you wish, but it will not replace you as the driver."
– Ayn Rand

When you make a dangerous amount of money and are feeling stuck or at an impasse, it helps to think about *why* you're focused on growing your wealth. What (or who) is the money ultimately for? What would having more money mean for your family and your quality of life? Looking ahead, what would your ideal week look like if you had all the money you'd ever need?

Since this is where I start with clients, it's where we're going to start this book: with you, thinking about your financial destination. The rest of this book is about the journey—how to steer around the hazards you may not even be recognizing right now as you speed through them. For now, though, I want you to spend a minute thinking about what it will be like when you finally "arrive."

In the very first meeting with a client, it's common practice for planners like me to ask people about their financial goals. While opening up about your relationship with money is never a bad thing, this is sometimes too large a question in a first meeting. Instead, I like to narrow the focus and ask you to think about your financial priorities.

That distinction—goals versus priorities—isn't just semantics. Understanding how they're different is the first step in building your own financial plan.

If I ask you, "What are your financial goals over the next twenty years?"—hopefully you can identify a few and explain why they matter to you. This is a GREAT start, as thinking about your goals is always a worthwhile exercise. But if we're ONLY focused on your goals, it leaves out a crucial detail: how important those goals are to you, relative to one another.

This is why I like to start the planning process by discussing your financial priorities.

When naming your goals, there's a tendency to see each item as an end in itself, which leaves no way for us to weigh how important one goal is in relation to another or to see how those various goals might impact each other. In other words, goals can provide direction and purpose, for sure, but **priorities** will help us decide which goals to focus on, and the best part: how to achieve them.

For example, if I ask you about your goals, you might answer with any number of the following:

- I want to retire in my late fifties.
- I want to buy a vacation home.
- I want to establish and fund a donor-advised fund for charitable giving.
- I want to send my kids to the colleges of their choice . . . without any debt.
- I want to start a business and know that I can go three years without my current salary.
- I want to give myself and my partner a year-long sabbatical so we can reset our lives.
- I want to double my travel budget for the next ten years.

Well, those are all meaningful and thoughtful *goals.* (All goals, if decided upon intentionally and honestly, are GREAT goals!) But most people don't have the money or resources to do everything they want (especially as they get more and more comfortable with their increasing lifestyle and the corresponding aspirations).

Desires and possibilities expand, and as they do, determining which of those goals are actual *priorities* is a huge part of making sure you are on the right track.

In practice, this means identifying HOW MUCH you want to achieve each of your goals and then organizing them in some sort of hierarchy based on what's MOST important to you.

Which goal are you most motivated by? Which would be "nice to have," but you're okay letting go if necessary (maybe because you thought about it for the first time eight minutes ago)? What do you consider to be non-negotiable (maybe because it's something that you and your partner have been talking about for a decade)? Maybe you have a goal you thought was super important, but once you hold it up to the light, you realize it doesn't make sense with everything else in your plans, and you scrap it. Maybe as these conversations progress, you narrow in on the one goal that's lost its luster over the years, so you're willing to sacrifice if it means achieving financial independence (as your family has defined it) sooner as a result.

Put simply, understanding your financial priorities (the ordering and layering of your financial goals upon one another) is where the real planning starts.

These conversations help us hone in on what you value most—which may not line up with what other people want, or even what you yourself once wanted. Understanding your genuine priorities takes focus and a willingness to keep asking questions and being honest about your answers. If I may be self-serving here, I also think it requires an objective third party to keep the conversation on the right track—especially if you're married, because marriage means there are three sets of priorities on the table: yours, your spouse's, and those you share.

Of course, I can't do all of that for you here. But I can get you started by giving you a taste of how Drucker Wealth helps our mid-career professional clients set their priorities and how we go about plotting a course to achieve them.

Our role? To help you define and articulate your goals, to ask detailed and thought-provoking questions, to attach tangible costs to your aspirations, and to look at your goals side-by-side. The result transforms a pie-in-the-sky "goals" list into a fully imagined set of scenarios—and from there, you can see what's possible and what it will take to make it happen.

Let's take one goal as an example. A client tells us they want to buy a vacation home for their growing family.

We start by asking questions like:

- When would you be looking to buy this home?
- What's the range you're thinking of spending?

Then we dig a little deeper:

- Are you thinking that it might ultimately become your primary residence?
- Would you rent it out while you're not there? Is this feasible?
- How much of the year would you stay there?
- Would your work support you staying there longer if you wanted to?

Our job is to unpack all of it, but, quite frankly, answering those questions and defining those costs is just baseline work. At this point, we're still establishing the foundation.

What comes next is what planning is all about.

We might ask:

- Is it more important that you buy the home in three years (your specified date) or that your purchase price is $2M (the amount you told us)? In other words, is having a vacation home ASAP the priority? Or is your main driver to make sure it's the dream house you imagine, even if it takes an extra few years to get there?
- Would you be willing to cut back on your vacation budget if the home cut into some of those expenses? Can you get your kids and partner on board with that?

- How would you compare your desire for the vacation home with your target to retire three years early? How does thinking about each one make you feel?

And then, when you've had some room to breathe and think about all this, I might dig even deeper, trying to unpack why the vacation home has become your primary target, by asking:

- What does having a vacation home mean to you? When you imagine this vacation home, what's the FIRST thing that comes to mind?
- If, instead of buying this vacation home, you took $50K per year and traveled freely instead . . . would that feel as rewarding? As comforting? What would be missing?

(And by the way, I am absolutely not trying to talk anyone out of buying a home, when this happens. It's just a thought exercise and a conversation starter, designed to help people laser in on their core motivations while considering alternatives—if only to eliminate them as options! And in case you haven't worked with a financial advisor focused on life planning . . . no, I am not coming out and firing these questions at my client like I'm the world's most direct therapist. It's all just a normal conversation! I simply want to give the client an opportunity to explore these questions on their end while we're chatting.)

And the conversation often goes even further. Unpacking *why* it's so important to them to have this vacation home might lead to exciting planning conversations that extend far beyond that goal. To take an example from a real conversation with clients whose motivation to buy a vacation home centered on family: They wanted to ensure their kids and future grandchildren would have a place to be together. The mom had that growing up, with her grandparents' home serving as a sort of family retreat/homebase for her and all her cousins—and she loved it. Well, that strikes me as a fantastic reason to plan for this vacation home. And as they start saving money for their dream of having all the cousins sitting around the fireplace by the lake, I bet they'll feel a lot more comfortable making the sort of short-term sacrifices it might take to get there! (The planner in me can't help but add that our next conversation revolved around their legacy and estate planning, in light of what they value most.)

Simply put, we need to understand how each goal affects your other long-term financial motivations so that when we run through your various plan scenarios, we know we're working toward your specific priorities. We need to know which of your priorities are important for meeting your core values and where you have flexibility. Maybe you can see yourself going in a few different directions. That's fine! You would tell us this, and we would be able to provide the most helpful and beneficial recommendations for change.

I started this chapter by mentioning a question that I don't like asking. Well, let me end with two questions that I LOVE to ask:

- If you look back to today in ten, twenty, or even thirty years—what are the two most important things that had to have happened for you to know that you are living a meaningful, happy, and purpose-filled life?? (More time with your kids? Early retirement? Travel? Providing for your kids' college? Starting a business?)
- If you look back to today in two months, what do you NEED to have accomplished for this financial planning process to have been a success?

Think about your answers to these two questions. They will force you to always keep in mind what's most important to you and what you're most committed to taking care of next. Together, they serve as the tentpoles of your financial plan.

They also help us to avoid two of the most damaging financial psychoses that can damn us before we even really get started: comparing ourselves to people we know nothing about and giving *money* a job it cannot do.

3

Financial Freedom Is Knowing When You Have "Enough"

"The hardest financial skill is to get the goalposts to stop moving."
— Morgan Housel, *The Psychology of Money*

It's instinctive to compare our finances to the people around us: their cars, their house(s), the trips they take . . . and I would say that this impulse is especially loud for someone who doesn't have a solid understanding of their finances. Being unable to resist this urge, sometimes new clients will ask early in the process, "So, now that you see my 'stuff,' how am I doing relative to your other clients?" And in my answer, I'm ultimately trying to get them comfortable with the following idea: "If it turns out that you're on track to fully fund your goals, if you can keep living your current lifestyle, and if you will have no financial worries through retirement . . . do you really care?"

In other words, once you know your financial priorities and are working through a plan to realize them, well, you stop looking for external validation (as much) or comparing yourself, mindlessly, to the people around you.

Not letting your friends' and colleagues' finances have an impact on your own approach to money is the first step toward attaining true financial peace of mind. The second, and the more difficult of the two, is understanding that wealth *is* subjective, and the way you think about your financial health has very little to do with your net worth. We've met clients with $5M who felt like they were swimming upstream with no end in sight, and clients with less than $1M who felt like they were sailing smoothly to their destination.

And both of them were correct!

Recognizing why is crucial.

Happiness (as it relates to money) is more about having realistic, achievable expectations than about the numbers on a spreadsheet. There are plenty of financially unfulfilled multi-millionaires and millions of financially content middle-class Americans! The folks who have true financial peace of mind (whether they have $2M, $20M, or $200M) know they have "enough" to do everything they want in life, AND they have the awareness to know that this means they've already won the game.

Because they are working off a committed financial plan, they have bridged the gap between where they are today and where they want to go and are endlessly content for having done so. They have reached or, in the case of the mid-career professional families we work with, are on track to reaching the final level: financial independence.

Our definition of financial independence is simple: doing what you want, when you want, with whom you want, for as long as you want, without being dependent on a paycheck. It's being able to fund your goals and to live the life you want to live. That's it. That's how we define and measure financial success. Your net worth is just the means to make THAT your financial reality.

If, however, you're operating under the assumption that financial peace of mind can be found by reaching a target number (whether that's your income, net worth, home price, or anything else), I promise you, it will always elude you. Oh, you might get to your number . . . but then you'll realize that, actually, your real number is 50% more than you thought. Then it's another 25%. And so on and so forth. And you will always be chasing your tail.

There's some relevant research from Kitces.com (the largest and most influential content hub for financial planners) that supports this reflection about the relationship between money and contentedness. The study revealed that people at every income benchmark ($100K, $250K, $500K, $750K, etc.) believed they would be financially content—they would feel they had "enough"—if they only earned a little bit more money. In people's minds, they were so close to achieving everything they wanted—they just needed a little bit more!

What's the problem? The fact that EVERYONE, at every income band, thought this! So having "enough" income was always slightly out of reach, because the person making $750K thought the exact same way as the person making $250K.

We can safely eliminate the possibility that ALL of these people, at various income levels, are correct in their assessment that they just need a bit more income and then their life would "come together."

What else could explain this phenomenon then? What's the root of the problem?

I'll be honest. The first time I thought about this, the financial planner part of my brain took over, and I thought the (obvious) answer was simply that most people don't have a plan for what to do with their income (Invest? Contribute to a Roth IRA? Pay down their mortgage?). So, regardless of the number, they always felt unprepared to maximize it. It's a super left-brained Certified Financial Planner (CFP®) take on the issue.

And that's true, of course, but it's not the REAL answer. After recently listening to a presentation by the brilliant Carl Richards (whose Behavior Gap sketches run through the book and whom I HIGHLY recommend you follow), I learned that the answer is much simpler: People too often assign *money* a job that it fundamentally CANNOT do.

We all, unknowingly, ask *money* to solve issues in our lives that it can't possibly adequately address: personal relationships, physical health, work satisfaction, maximizing our time, etc. Subconsciously, we start to believe that more *money* is a cure for other, non-financial aspects of our lives and that it can increase our happiness quotient across the board.

It's a slippery slope when we assign money to these incredibly personal jobs. We start to think of things like:

- If I earn an extra $50K, I'll feel more appreciated at work, and therefore I'll be a happier person and be able to show up more for my friends.
- If I make more money, I'll feel better about the fact that I don't have as much time to work out and stay in shape as I'd like, AND I'll be able to pay for a nicer gym.

- If we have more money, we'll be able to spend more money on vacations, and our family will be happier spending time together.

These ideas are so intoxicating because if you squint, you can see them! You can understand how we all tell ourselves these things without even realizing we're doing it.

The problem, of course, is that once we hit this next level of income, we realize that the additional money didn't ultimately "solve" the underlying issue and, instead of wondering if maybe we're assigning money a job that it's not designed to do, it's easier to re-group and decide that it just wasn't ENOUGH money and so we try again!

I started this chapter with the Morgan Housel's quote, "The hardest financial skill is getting the goalpost to stop moving," because SO MUCH about developing a successful relationship with money is downstream of this message. Being comfortable talking about money and being honest about what money can do for you (and what it can't) is how you control and maximize it without letting it control you.

We'll end this section by simply reiterating our central point.

Focusing your money energies on:

- What John and Mary are doing down the street
- What you see on Instagram or in Financial Media
- That random Net Worth Number that "feels" like making it

. . . is a recipe to driving yourself crazy (without even anything positive to show for it!).

Having a financial plan based on *your* priorities and values, rather than on what others are doing, is THE best way to attain real financial peace of mind.

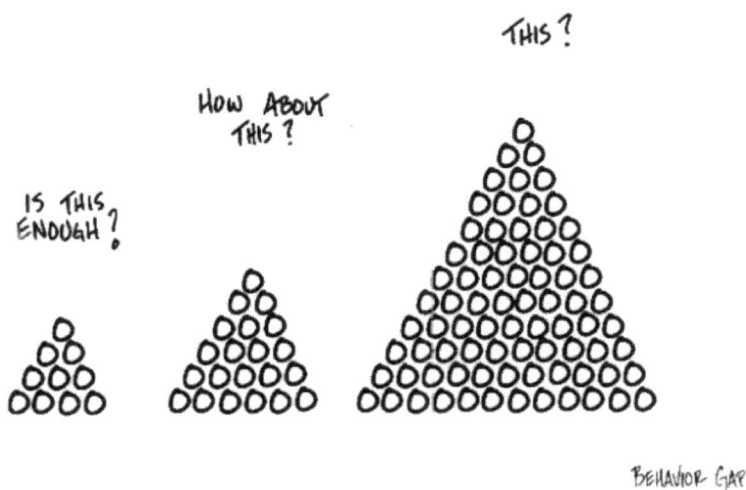

BEHAVIOR GAP

So . . . how do we get there? Intentionality, discipline, and steadfastness.

I am of the mind that *most* individuals and families would be best served by hiring a fiduciary financial planner to guide them through their financial journey, partner with them in their financial thinking, and hold them accountable. Before you roll your eyes—yes, I am biased! Like the doctor who sees their kid cough and imagines all the terrible things it could be, I've seen too much! I know that having a *real* fiduciary financial planner in your corner—and paying them to be there—will never be the reason you don't reach your financial goals, but not having one could absolutely be your downfall . . . and I consider everything else a detail. So, again, feel free to consider me "biased" in this perspective as the owner of a financial planning and wealth management firm. I can only share what I know from being part of a firm that spans three generations and has spent sixty-plus years guiding clients to financial independence.

By the end of this book, you'll have enough information and context to decide for yourself whether you want to hire a financial planner. Whatever you decide about what's right for your family is okay. Either way, if you work through this book, you will be more committed to tackling your financial future and more educated in deciding how to go about it . . . and I consider *that* a win.

4

Why Do We Plan When Your Life Is Constantly Changing?

"Planning is important, but the most important part of every plan is to plan on the plan not going according to plan."
— Morgan Housel

Early on in my career, I came across a quote from philosopher Carveth Read who said, "I would rather be vaguely right than precisely wrong."

At the time, I couldn't put my finger on it, but it seemed like a big part of what I was starting to do for clients. And then a few years later, I heard Carl Richards say, "Financial planning is not about being precisely right today . . . it's about being less wrong tomorrow," and it all clicked.

When we first start working with clients, we do so knowing full well that unexpected life events will change the plan assumptions we're using and the plan outcomes we're working toward. We know your life will not pan out *exactly* as you lay it out during the planning process. In fact, life hardly *ever* goes as planned.

Unfortunately, many people never create their financial roadmap because they believe they'll never have ALL the information necessary to be "precisely" right (which is true)—and so they throw the baby out with the bathwater. They never even get started, and as a result, they lose out on the peace of mind and confidence that come from being "vaguely right" (or as I like to say, "directionally correct").

Another relevant truism: **"Perfect is the enemy of good."**

I've seen people get so bogged down by the success probabilities of their financial plan, or so obsessed over their initial plan assumptions, that they paralyze themselves. They become unable to make the financial decisions necessary to improve their standing. In their quest for 100% certainty, they miss out on becoming 20% better today than they were yesterday.

For these types of people, putting together a financial plan can be difficult to wrap their heads around.

It's not the cost that stops them.

It's not the financial terms or the emotional pitfalls embedded in money conversations.

It's not about having to go through their expenses or think about a potential injury or unexpected death.

No—some people just have a really difficult time with planning around "uncertainty."

Putting together a financial plan is like putting together a big jigsaw puzzle. Truthfully, it can best be described as putting together a big jigsaw puzzle *while missing a bunch of important pieces.* And just like if you were to do a puzzle without all the pieces, we have to be comfortable with the idea that we can make important strides AND that it will not be perfect or fit together seamlessly. These two facts are not at odds.

Why?

Because when we complete the actual financial planning work—assessing current and future cash flows, mapping out retirement probabilities, discussing alternate housing and education scenarios—we are doing so with an unknowable future. We don't know exactly how much money you'll make in five years, what type of college your kid(s) will go

29

to, what the market will do over the next decade, whether your company/job will stay the same, or even whether you'll want to retire when you reach that stage of life.

This can be crazy-making for overly analytical clients (typically "engineering"-brained folks, if I can throw my brother-in-law and his colleagues under the bus). They can get so wrapped up in our (and their own) analysis that they start to obsess over tiny details of future outcomes that haven't materialized yet. They get so stuck on elements of the plan that don't truly matter, while ignoring the components that do.

I recently designed a financial plan with a family who reached out for the first time a year before we eventually got started. On that first call, I recall the husband, John, telling me that he'd never completed a financial plan because he felt it always seemed kind of crazy to do so before he really had all the relevant numbers "at hand." I remember asking him, a bit tongue-in-cheek, when he thought he would have those figures and therefore be ready to begin.

He got the point.

While he was waiting to have all the "inputs" ready, he had missed opportunities (low-hanging fruit, as it were) to make tactical improvements and make his future a little less hazy.

That's what planning is all about. It's sketching a picture of the future in broad outlines so that over time, we can color between the lines. Planning is just as much about the important questions that linger as it is about the way you answer at that moment in time.

Questions like:

- What are you building wealth for?
- How do you want to spend your wealth later?
- How can your money be used for maximum happiness for your family right now?
- How are you going to be taxed later?

Your plan serves as your roadmap. It's a way for us to eliminate as many future surprises as possible by taking action and adjusting as necessary over time.

Of course, no plan, based on an unknowable future, can be perfect . . . but as long as you approach planning with the right mindset, there's no one I've ever met who wouldn't be better served by having a financial plan put in place yesterday. If only they could get out of their own way.

If you're reading this book, you likely understand that in a life of uncertainty:

- Being "vaguely right" is the marker of success.
- Getting on the right track is the benchmark.
- Becoming even 10% more financially secure with each passing year is a home run.

So, if "the plan" is just a starting point, an ever-evolving mechanism, why is it so important to have one guiding your financial behavior?

Because when your life evolves . . . say if:

- You get married and have kids sooner than expected.
- You get an exciting new job opportunity.
- You decide to move across the country.
- You need to help your folks with their financial affairs.

We will already have your financial blueprint in place, so the work is just to *update* and *adjust* the plan, rather than frustratingly starting from scratch with each new development. Financial planning—and my team's role, should we work together—is about making adjustments to what already works, rather than reinventing the wheel with each passing year.

Simply put, we are your GPS. And, once we have your priorities sorted out (as described in Chapter 2), we will keep you moving in the right direction. We will help you understand how the minutiae of your life affect the ultimate destination you've hired us to help you reach.

What I'm saying is this: Making a right turn is a heck of a lot easier when you've already gotten into your car and started driving!

When you have a plan in place, you've done the hard part: You're moving forward.

Don't wait to get started just because the timing isn't "right." There is no perfect time to build a financial plan in a world where your life is constantly evolving. A "pretty good" plan that you update periodically is a whole lot better than no plan at all!

5

Retirement Planning Is Harder Than It Used to Be

"The question isn't at what age I want to retire, it's at what income."
– George Foreman

A big reason I wrote this book (and why I work with mid-career professionals in the first place) is that retirement planning is objectively more complicated than ever before. In this chapter, I want to touch on the "how/why" of this unfortunate reality, because it's important to understand the work we have ahead of us. Every other chapter in this book will then provide you with the strategies, concepts, and decision-making prowess to do something about it.

The first thing I want to note is that when I say "retirement planning," I don't just mean the traditional idea of retiring at sixty-five and sitting on a beach. To my mid-career professionals, retirement is shorthand for financial independence. Nothing less and nothing more. Remember our definition? Doing what you want, with whom you want, for as long as you want, while not being dependent on a paycheck. Retirement planning, therefore, is about living the life you want now, while you're working, and later, when you're not. It means striking the right balance between your current desires and lifestyle and your future needs. It could mean aiming to retire at fifty or "semi"-retiring at fifty-five and powering down gradually. It could mean retiring at seventy because you *want* to keep working, not because you need to. Or it could mean that your retirement age isn't that important to you because you're driven by other priorities and goals. All of this is "retirement planning."

Okay, enough preamble. Let's get started with a question: What is the number one reason retirement is more difficult now than it's ever been?

Answer: Very, very few of us are fortunate enough to have a pension. If the word "pension" is new to you, or you've heard of it but have no idea what it means, let me explain. A pension, which was a staple of twentieth-century retirement planning, was a fantastic retirement vehicle. Pensions provided a guaranteed monthly retirement benefit for the rest of your life. For example: If you worked forty years as a public-school teacher, you would receive a monthly paycheck equivalent to 80–90% of your three highest-earning years . . . *for the rest of your life*, after you turned sixty-five and retired.

As you might imagine, retirement planning becomes a heck of a lot easier if you have a lifetime income stream that replaces most of your working income. There's not that much of an income gap to fill! But over the course of the last forty years, this has all changed. Apparently, these pension plans have become too expensive for companies (and schools and the government, for that matter) to maintain, and while they still exist today, they've mostly been phased out or reduced.

What took their place? Well, these days, most of us are tasked with funding our OWN retirement. This is essentially what the government and employers told us by creating and emphasizing the 401(k) retirement plan. Unlike a pension, a 401(k) (and a 403b, TSP, 457, etc.) is a defined contribution plan. There is NO guaranteed income stream in retirement, there is no guaranteed interest, *there is no guaranteed anything.* However much money you choose to put into your 401(k) each year, and however much it grows based on the investment allocation you've chosen—that's how much money you will have in your 401(k) by the time you need to access it (and, yes, maybe there's a match to your annual contributions along the way).

If you hit the 401(k) hard in your first five years of retirement, there very well may not be anything left for the later stages of retirement. (Again, compare this to the beauty of a pension in which you receive a monthly check of $5K *indefinitely.* Even if you live to be ninety-five years old, that check just keeps coming.)

So, it's clear that when we're tasked with saving for our own retirement, retirement planning becomes a lot more important than it was when we could slide right from our careers into retirement with nary a change in guaranteed income. We all need to ensure that we are adequately funding our 401(k)s, Roth IRAs, HSAs, taxable investment accounts, after-tax 401(k)s, and so on—because the moment we stop working or sell our business, we may not have a dime of income to replace that former paycheck.

This is part of why the projected estimates for an adequate retirement nest egg for our forty-year-old clients are significantly more substantial than for those who are already sixty-five years old. If you're sixty-five and receiving a monthly check of $4K per month from your pension and $3K from Social Security, it may only take a net worth of $1M to $2M to fill the income gap and for you to feel comfortable for the rest of your life.

For many of our younger, high-earning clients . . . *this won't even come close to cutting it.*

So, what's my point? The work has to start earlier. We have to be more *intentional* and *purposeful* with our saving habits, our investment process, and our spending goals over the years.

And if retirement means giving yourself the option to become work-life optional as early as you want, you also have to make sure you're not JUST saving into a 401(k) (or 403b, TSP, SEP IRA, or other similar employer-sponsored plans), because you only begin to have access to those accounts at age fifty-nine and a half.

For our clients, becoming work-life optional might look like moving from their high-paying, high-stress corporate job at fifty-two to work part-time or in a consulting capacity until age sixty—even if that means making a substantially lower sum. If this kind of early "retirement" is part of your plan, you're going to need to distribute some of your assets before you're fifty-nine and a half—so we'd better make sure you have adequate investment accounts NOT held in a 401(k).

Don't get me wrong, 401(k)s are a wonderful and necessary savings vehicle. Most of the clients we work with are maxing them out to the fullest extent possible and should be. But a 401(k) alone does not help with the specific goal of early retirement because you will be penalized for taking money out if you're younger than fifty-nine and a half. (We will get A LOT more into retirement account structures in Part 3 . . . this just seemed a necessary detour given our mention of early retirement.)

And the pension/401(k) "bait and switch" is only *half* of why the roadmap has changed so dramatically over the last fifteen years. The second piece of this "problem" is actually a wonderful thing, though it comes with financial challenges. It's increased longevity. People are living a lot longer than ever before and, as a result, need to stretch their assets to last longer.

Simply put, we have our work cut out for us.

6

Financial Advice is Changing (For the Better!)

"Budgeting is telling your money where to go, instead of wondering where it went."
— John Barnes

This chapter might be the most important one in the entire book, as it addresses a widespread misconception that has prevented thousands of high-earning professionals from receiving the financial guidance they desperately need.

To put it plainly: Parts of the financial services industry have operated under a broken model for a long time. This isn't just frustrating—it's fundamentally backward. Let me explain why we're in the midst of a financial planning revolution that's finally putting the focus where it belongs.

The world of professional financial advice has undergone significant changes over the last five to ten years. I'd argue that it's going through a revolution of sorts . . . and mid-career individuals and families like yours will be better served as a result.

Once upon a time, when financial advisors spoke about financial planning, they just meant "investment management." Even more egregiously, some of these "financial advisors" just meant "let me sell you an insurance policy you don't need." (This seems like a relevant time to highlight the fact that ANYONE can call themselves a financial advisor. There is no barrier to doing so. In the fourth section of this book, we'll discuss how to find a *real* fiduciary financial planner.)

Most "financial plans" were offered for free (if wealth advisors thought to pay lip service to the idea of financial planning at all), because the real goal was to invest the client's available funds once the plan was complete.

Why would they provide a real, actionable plan if it meant more work prior to investing and a delay to the one thing they did want to do—charge a fee to manage investments? And in the mind of the client, who had been conditioned to think that financial advice was just another commodity where the lowest price tag wins and that investment management was synonymous with real financial planning, why *wouldn't* they say yes to a financial plan they didn't have to pay for (at least not up front)?

Unfortunately, twenty years ago, we, as an industry, conflated the ideas of (1) financial planning and (2) investment management to such an astounding degree that the public began to believe the two were one and the same. A financial "advisor's" primary role was to gather investment assets, manage those specific accounts, and make changes to the accounts as necessary, and they were compensated specifically—and only—for that function.

As a result, both advisors and the public came to the implicit understanding that investment management was worth paying for and financial planning advice was not. This meant that only people with a substantial investment portfolio could work with a financial advisor, and too often, even these folks wouldn't get comprehensive planning.

This misguided idea has permeated the culture. I am always floored when I hear in casual conversation, "I don't have enough money to have a financial advisor." This logic is fundamentally backward!

Because . . . really? In what universe does it follow that unless you already have a few million to invest, you can't possibly have questions about:

- Your cash flow and budgeting
- Tax planning and your annual tax liability
- Your kids' education planning and goals
- Your benefits, stock options, and retirement accounts at work
- Your protection and insurance planning
- Your student loans and broader strategy to pay off debt
- Pre-tax Roth versus after-tax prioritization
- Estate planning and legacy coordination
- Quantifying your financial behavior
- Analyzing your housing costs and real estate expectations
- Long-term scenario planning

YOUR COMPLETE FINANCIAL LIFE

YOUR INVESTMENTS

BEHAVIOR GAP

Are we really saying that a couple in their early forties, earning $450K, with three kids, twenty-seven goals, and twelve financial/estate/tax questions should wait until they have millions before they're able to benefit from—and pay for—professional financial advice? That is both insane and counterproductive. In fact, they are in the group that MOST needs real financial advice! Without it, they're setting themselves up to be like Marc and Laura—the clients I mentioned at the beginning of the book—marching toward a "dangerous amount of income," without any real insight as to how they're doing, what they can afford to be doing, and how to reach their intended financial destination.

And this is why advisors started setting asset management minimums (i.e.: "we only work with you if you have $2M of investments for us to manage."). For clients with smaller account balances, there was no way for many advisors to be adequately compensated otherwise. These advisors couldn't charge for financial planning independently of the assets they managed since they weren't really *doing* financial planning and people would wonder what they're paying for!

That reality has now changed. But the legacy of those days is millions of people not receiving or paying for financial advice because they were either embarrassed that they didn't yet have millions to invest or so put off by their initial conversations with financial advisors—which immediately jumped to finding out how much money they could or would invest—that they vowed never to speak to one again!

And so, receiving financial planning advice became the domain of people who already had substantial net worth and were approaching retirement. (Why retirees? Because, as Willie Sutton once said about robbing banks, *that's where the money is!* The older you are, the greater the likelihood you'll have acquired assets in need of being managed.)

(As an aside: Even this is backward! People in retirement have substantially *fewer* life transitions that require financial planning than people in their mid-career years. Mid-career families, meanwhile, are worried about family planning, education funding, home purchase planning, funding family vacations, changing careers, combining family finances, saving enough for eventual retirement, and so on.)

Zooming out, the problem is not that financial advisors were charging too much in fees . . . not at all. I want and deserve to be paid for the excellent financial advice and wealth management services my team and I provide to the families that rely on us. (In fact, we don't want to be—and are not—the lowest cost option. We want to be the solution providing the most VALUE.) The problem is that too many advisors aren't providing genuine planning advice or integrating tax, estate, and charitable giving into their offerings for the families who already pay them for this sort of comprehensive help. The truth is that most of the older-school, big-box firms that created the current dynamic are just not set up to tackle those areas of planning.

Well, Drucker Wealth *is* set up for this. In fact, it's our exact program. (And by the way, there are a number of other fantastic *independent* fiduciary financial planning firms that are also changing the concept of financial planning.) And while our firm's new clients now do have more than $1M+ in investment assets, there are plenty of excellent fiduciary firms that work with clients even earlier in their financial journey than we do. My point in castigating the industry for not being set up to help younger/less wealthy clients isn't to say that every firm needs to be able to help everyone, only that there should be firms out there to serve every type of client AND that engage in real financial planning . . . and now there are!

Let's walk through what this sort of planning looks like in practice. We call this our Financial Life Plan® program, and every single one of our new clients goes through it with us BEFORE we manage any investments. (By the way, I debated moving this section explaining my firm's process to the section of the book about hiring a planner. In the end, it seemed necessary to include here, if only as an example to really understand the way financial advice has changed and what this means as you approach the rest of the concepts laid out in the pages to come.)

As you have no doubt gathered from the first few chapters of this book, our team specializes in helping high-earning individuals and families in their late thirties and forties design a personalized financial roadmap by prescribing tactical and behavioral changes to bring them closer to their long-term financial goals. We charge a fee for this initial engagement and strive to address all their financial, tax, and estate particulars over a two-month planning period. At the plan's conclusion, our clients can choose to take their plan with all the advice we have provided and implement the recommendations on their own, or they can hire us to serve as their ongoing financial planner and wealth advisor . . . the choice is entirely up to them!

Only once we have reached the end of the initial engagement—when we're all more organized and clearer on both the big picture and the details—do we start discussing our ongoing investment management services and planning the next steps. And because this happens at the end of the plan, by the time we get to this stage of the relationship, most clients WANT to move on to the ongoing comprehensive services (which include investment management and tax prep) because they've already seen the way we work and the value we provide.

We'll continue this conversation in the book's last section, exploring how to find the right financial planner for your family (it might not be us!). For now, we're left to ask a question: If asset level isn't the deciding factor in when you should hire a financial planner . . . what *is*?

It's **household income**. (I know this is the second time I've asked a question and provided an immediate answer

. . . what can I say? Our audience doesn't have the time to wait three paragraphs for the answer!)

This realization, along with the reality that thousands of households are now getting the help and advice they need (and deserve), is the start of a new era in financial planning advice.

A certain level of annual household income will create enough complexity, opportunity, competing cash-flow priorities, and the means to fund your goals that you will be best served by having a great financial planner in your corner.

In the next chapter, we will explain why, as your advisory team, we consider a high household income the clearest indicator that we can make meaningful and substantial financial changes for you.

7

Financial Planning for Mid-Career Professionals

"Money is, in some respects, like fire. It is a very excellent servant, but a terrible master."
— P. T. Barnum

We now know that "net worth" and "money to invest" are the wrong metrics to use as you start thinking about whether you could benefit from professional financial advice and organization.

Instead—for those in their thirties and forties, especially—household income is the indicator for when you would benefit from getting more intentional and proactive about your financial decision-making, because with a higher income, you have the cash flow to think beyond the present. I hesitate to give a number here because a "high" income depends on location and cost of living (and the level of financial planning support and services you need). For example, making $175K while living in Florida is different than making $175K and living in San Francisco or New York. For us—a comprehensive full-service planning firm—it's individuals who make $200K+ and dual-income households earning $350K+.

As we stated earlier, financial planning is about balancing your current wants with your future needs. A big part of our job, therefore, is helping our clients maximize their current lifestyle, experiences, and quality of life while making sure it doesn't negatively impact their ability to attain financial independence in the future. And naturally, the more income you have, the more decisions there are to make and the more context and help you need to avoid swinging that balance too far in either direction.

This is why a high income (a.k.a. "making a dangerous amount of money") is the dividing line: A high enough income allows you to think beyond the day-to-day financial concerns of your household. You can look up and start thinking about the competing uses of your money and the balance between your present and future concerns. You have the means and motivation to think beyond just "living life" each year, and you can start imagining and planning for the as-yet-undetermined future. When you've reached this point, new questions, concerns, opportunities, and strategies start to present themselves. This is where a Certified Financial Planner (CFP®) comes in.

To that end, here's a (partial) list of questions and concepts a CFP® will advise on once your income allows for it. By the way, these questions are just as important to answer if you have zero intention of ever hiring a financial planner and want to do it all yourself. That's fine, too! This book will tell you what a real financial planner will explore and emphasize—and if you aren't going to hire one, then *you* need to play the role instead!

- What should your savings rate be? In other words, what percentage of your household income needs to be saved for you to hit your targeted financial goals?
- Are your financial goals achievable based on your current income, time horizon, and existing assets? What needs to change to make them feasible?

- More specifically, when is the best time to target these goals? Should you buy a vacation home in five years, or would that deplete your cash/investment reserves to an unhealthy degree? Does it make more sense to buy a less expensive home or to defer buying that home for an extra few years?

- When looking at your savings potential, how do we prioritize those savings to help you become more tax-efficient in your overall asset allocation? Are you using the right mix of pre-tax retirement accounts, backdoor Roth IRAs, After-tax 401(k)s, taxable investment contributions, health savings accounts (HSAs)/ flexible spending accounts, supplemental executive retirement plans (SERPs), cash accumulation, 529 education vehicles, and so on?

- Is it the right time in your life to convert existing pre-tax accounts into Roth accounts? Will doing so bump you into a higher tax bracket or keep you at the same level? What are your personal expectations and philosophy for income trajectory and tax rates over time?

- If you have children, what are the best saving vehicles for your specific goals (e.g., 529 accounts, custodial accounts, taxable accounts, and trusts)? How much should you be saving for your children versus saving toward your retirement?

- Are you maximizing your retirement/health options through work? Does your firm have an after-tax 401(k), an HSA, a deferred comp plan, or pension benefits? Do you understand how they impact your plan?

- Are you making the most strategic decisions with your stock options? How should you think about your Restricted Stock Units (RSUs) in the context of your broader income? What is an appropriate amount of concentration to have in company equity given your age, income, and investing time horizon?

- If you are in a new marriage/relationship, how do you start merging your finances with your partner? Is it necessary/important to set up joint investment accounts, or can accounts remain separate while goals are combined?

- Have you done a sufficient job of protecting your current income and your future income potential via various insurance coverages (e.g., disability, life, or long-term care)? Most high-income earners are vastly underinsured, especially if they rely solely on their employer-sponsored plans.

- Do you have a proper estate plan set up if you were to pass away prematurely? Do you have a will and a health care proxy? Have you chosen guardians, trustees, and fiduciaries who can handle your assets?

- Are your existing retirement accounts and investments allocated in a way that makes the most sense for you from a risk, tax-efficiency, cost, and performance standpoint? Why do you own what you own inside of your retirement accounts?

- Do you have a purposeful program for paying off debt (e.g., student loans, mortgages, or personal loans) that takes into account interest rates, liquidity, and your personal comfort level? Why do we talk about "good" debts versus "bad" debts?

- If you want to be able to help your parents as they get older, are there vehicles and ways to title your accounts that let you take care of your spouse and kids *and* your own parents?

- If you have 401(k)s from seven different companies and you're not sure where they are or how they're set up, could you use help in establishing a clear and purposeful approach toward these retirement dollars?

- If the market's volatility is causing you anxiety, but you're not sure how it affects you given your current investment allocation . . . how would a complete analysis of your existing accounts and a better understanding of historical trends prepare you to weather the next market correction?

None of these questions and areas of focus are less important to answer or any less relevant to your family if you have $500K to invest instead of $5M. In fact, having answers to these questions is substantially more valuable if you're younger, because the value you receive will have more time to compound (just like the money itself) for your future. You get more time to let all the changes work in your favor!

8

Personal Finance Is More Personal Than It Is Finance

"Spending money to show people how much money you have is the fastest way to have less money."
– Morgan Housel

One of my favorite money maxims is personal finance is way more "personal" than it is finance.[1] Unlike other areas of finance where everything important happens on (and can be explained by) a spreadsheet, personal finance happens at the dinner table, on vacation, and, crucially, is made up of hundreds of decisions, big and small. In this way personal finance is more like running a business than anything else. With that in mind, I ask every potential new client I meet: ***Can you see yourself, by yourself, treating your family's finances the same way you might organize a business?***

Treating something like a business means:

- Having a mission and taking it seriously
- Having processes and procedures in place to get results
- Having clear definitions of success
- Being able to separate out the "personal" and "emotional" from the "professional"

Anything that is treated with such purpose and intentionality is going to have a much higher chance of success. And doesn't your family's financial future deserve this type of thinking and coordination?

If you can answer four out of the five following questions with a "yes," I would say you and your family are being appropriately intentional and objective about the way you run your financial household.

1. Do you have regular scheduled meetings with your spouse to discuss recent financial happenings in your family's situation?

2. Do you go through your family's numbers each year to make sure the business (i.e., your family's finances) is secure? Examples may include discussing your next two to three years of income expectations, as well as your savings rate, net-worth growth, insurance protection, or education funding targets.

3. Do you build out one-year, five-year, and twenty-year goals for what you're looking to achieve as a family?

4. Do you have open and honest conversations about your financial decision-making and how it has changed over time?

5. Do you have policies and procedures to make sure you and your spouse are addressing different aspects of your financial foundation on a regular basis?

These questions might seem funny or ridiculous in the context of a married couple (they do to me!). C'mon, you're probably thinking to yourself, "*Do you really expect my husband and me to sit down at the kitchen table and talk to each other like business partners during the twenty minutes between picking the kids up from soccer and cooking dinner? Do you expect my wife and me to hand each other a financial report card when we get into bed to watch Netflix at night?*"

No . . . I don't! I think attempting to do this on your own is almost impossible. And that's exactly my point. One of the most important reasons families hire a financial planner is to have someone external—an impartial third party—who forces them to have detailed, specific, and sensitive conversations about money on a regular basis. We provide an open forum for these conversations to take place, while we listen and translate them into real, tangible action steps.

To show how this works, I'll share a recent client meeting I had with Janie and Bryan.

We had just completed their initial planning engagement and were moving on to the ongoing phase of the relationship, so the meeting included a few logistical, next-step details. A big part of the conversation over the preceding few months had been around their desire to buy a new home, since they had just moved across the country and were renting while they figured things out and got their kids settled at school.

I asked Janie if the plan was still to buy a home in the next six months, and she said something like, "Ah, I've been thinking about that a lot recently! Now that we've been living here a few months, we are so much happier than we thought we'd be! We love our neighbors, the kids get along so well with the other kids on the block, and honestly, I'm just not in as much of a rush to move as I thought I would be!"

Bryan, her husband, immediately stared at her and said, "Wait, really? When did this happen? You were the one who wanted to move ASAP!"

They both looked at me and laughed. Then two things happened:

1. I told them that I was IMMEDIATELY adding this story, word-for-word, to my book.
2. Bryan joked that this five-minute conversation validated our fees for the next five years.

Without a financial planner organizing you and taking the initiative, conversations like this—and the action steps they make possible—may simply never happen. Maybe that's not true across the board. For instance, retired people may have all the time in the world to focus on their finances—but it is absolutely true of the clients I work with. Most of my clients have some combination of the following profiles:

- One or two working parent(s) in the "middle" of high-stress careers with minimal personal time
- Single high-income earners who travel a lot and have ZERO free time Variable income, whether in the form of RSUs, target bonuses, or performance bonuses
- Thinking about buying a vacation home or a larger primary residence

If this sounds like you, then you probably know better than anybody: Do you really have the time and energy to sit down and figure out an automated investment program? Or your disability insurance needs? Or when and how often to rebalance your 401(k) portfolio? Of course not! You're too busy going to soccer practice and then rushing to a dance recital before putting the kids to sleep so you can work on a presentation you're supposed to give at work on Friday.

The idea that you're going to fit a disciplined and comprehensive financial planning process into that chaos is just not realistic. Fortunately, it's also not necessary. Real financial planners (like those on my team) love helping busy families who operate at a breakneck speed! Seeing the visible sigh of relief when people realize they don't have to go it alone or keep "putting it off" is truly the highlight of my week.

There is nothing more satisfying for me than putting a financial plan into place for individuals and families like this. Once my clients realize they have a partner who will keep their eyes on the prize, they can go out and live their lives . . . and actually enjoy them.

One last thing worth noting: I know from my clients that an underappreciated and unexpected benefit of review meetings with an advisor is the opportunity, a handful of times per year, to step back from the day-to-day grind and think about the bigger picture: what they've accomplished, where they're headed, and how they feel about it all. It may sound corny (and of course, not every review meeting does this) but knowing that you have forty-five minutes coming up next month where your fiduciary planner is going to ask about your life vision, your financial priorities, and your career trajectory can absolutely serve as a catalyst for change.

9

Real Financial Planning: Where Do You Start?

"And since you can build wealth without a high income, but have no chance of building it without a high savings rate, it's clear which one matters more."

– Morgan Housel

If I could only know one fact about your family's finances before determining whether you were on the right track to accomplishing your financial goals, what do you think it would be?

You would probably expect it to be one of the "big" numbers, like your income, your 401(k) balance, or the value of your home . . . right? Nope, nope, and definitely not! (More on this exclamation later.)

It's your **savings rate**.

Your savings rate tells me more about your current and future financial health than any other number we can possibly look at. By "savings rate," I mean the percentage of your gross household income that you save each year, encompassing money that you add to your retirement accounts, investment accounts, bank accounts, 529s, and any other investment vehicles you might own.

One important point to make now is this: Your savings rate does *not* include money you might not be spending today but will spend months from now. That's just deferred spending! Money included in your savings rate is money you are putting aside with no specific/recognized cost attached to it, simply because you have a reasonable expectation that this money will be worth more to you in the future than it is right now.

We've had clients with a household income of $600K, whose financial plans were hanging by a thread. Their lifestyle and future goals had become so outlandishly large that they were only saving 8–10% of their gross income each year. With huge, fixed expenses and expensive future goals, their 10% savings rate ($60K annually) was not going to allow them to build a nest egg that could one day replace the $600K in income they were currently living on. Sometimes, it really is that simple.

On the flip side, we've had clients earning half that income ($300K annually), but with a 25% savings rate, they're putting aside $75K annually!

Who do you think is in better long-term financial shape? And that's to say nothing of the fact that the second family will likely need less income in retirement to satisfy their financial goals because they're already living on less money in the first place.

In this way, retirement planning is sometimes a two birds, one stone situation: **If you save more money, you will (1) have more money in the future and (2) become used to saving so much (and therefore spending less) that you will also require less money to satisfy your needs in the future.** This, my friends, is a recipe for financial freedom!

Now that we have established that solving your savings rate is the starting point for your financial health, the next most important questions we seek to answer revolve around your cash flow, as this will help us determine your target savings rate.

Here are the three questions we want to be able to answer at the end of the planning process (and then each year moving forward):

1. How much excess saving capacity do you have after all your expenses are taken care of?

2. What percentage of your gross income does this saving capacity equate to (i.e., what is your savings rate)?

3. Will saving/investing this amount of money allow you to reach your specific financial goals?

To answer these questions, we first need to figure out how you spend your money month to month. We start by uncovering and unpacking your *fixed expenses*. These are expenses you absolutely must spend every month to live and which are relatively static, such as rent/mortgage, groceries, subscriptions, car payments, and so on.

Next, we figure out your *variable expenses*. (These are more discretionary: going-out money, travel, random purchases, Amazon, gifts, etc.) We talk about what your one-off "big" purchases will look like over the next few years (for instance, vacations, school payments, buying a ring/planning a wedding, down payment on a home, or buying a car). At the start, we need to know what these numbers look like now and how they've moved (directionally) over time.

Why is it so important to do this first part? Because after we go through all of your "stuff" (your salary; bonus; stock options; RSUs; the money going into your 401[k]s; the money being allocated for federal, state, local taxes; health insurance; HSAs; etc.), we will show you exactly how much money you *currently* have left over to "save" each month. *Currently* is the key word here, because this part isn't about understanding what your savings rate should be or will become. We'll get there. The first step is simply knowing what money is realistically available based on your current lifestyle.

Once we've gone through all of this, we'll have a better answer for those first two questions.

1. We'll know your current **saving capacity** in actual dollar amounts per month (and what you have left over).

2. We'll know your **savings rate** as a percentage of your household income.

Of course, once we've made sense of your current cash flow, sometimes it IS my job to bring clients to the realization that they have to make big changes to get where they want to go.

Maybe their monthly fixed expenses are so high that they're pushing their dreams of early retirement further away. Maybe their dual goals of buying a bigger house and sending their kids to a private high school would drastically reduce the success rate of their plan because they would no longer be able to save 25+% of their gross income. Maybe the idea of semi-retiring at age fifty and reducing their income from $350K to $75K for ten years after that is exciting to think about, but it would require substantial behavioral changes to make it feasible.

I know that sometimes, the moment calls for these conversations. In fact, this is what the client is paying us to help them understand—and then rectify. So this is always the first step of the planning process with Drucker Wealth clients, all of whom earn $350K+ in household income and have accumulated between $1M and $5M in investment assets when they first meet us. I repeat this client profile because, unfortunately, as we've seen, these fantastic income/asset figures do not actually tell me whether a change or reframe will need to be made.

That would be a depressing end to the chapter, wouldn't it? Luckily, that's not the last thing to say about expenses and savings. You might find it hard to believe, but we spend just as much time helping clients *spend* their money as we do helping them to save, grow, and protect it. Just as over-spending can be a problem . . . so can underspending! The purpose of financial planning and being financially disciplined is not to wait until you're eighty years old to enjoy your money!

The point of being aware of your spending behavior is that doing so frequently gives people MORE "permission" to spend more money, take more trips, and splurge more often, because they know their numbers, their limits, and where they have wiggle room!

Put another way, a lot of people feel anxious or stressed about money, not because they're spending too much, but because they just have no idea . . . and when we don't have enough information, we tend to assume the worst. It's the uncertainty of it all, not the spending, that is usually the problem.

Once we've shown clients how much they're saving and how their net worth is growing, we indirectly (and sometimes directly!) give them the freedom to spend without guilt—while still feeling more confident about their money decisions overall, thanks to the targeted savings program we set them up with. It's freeing, not restrictive.

To that end, I recently had the good fortune of telling one of our client households, Jake and Stephanie, that they could (no, let me rephrase that . . . they *should*) spend an extra $5K on a vacation that year. In fact, I told them to book their next trip as soon as we got off the phone. I was ecstatic to share with them that their plan looked incredible and all the scenarios they had asked us to show were working to an overwhelming degree. Stephanie and Jake were each in their early forties. Here's what their plan showed:

- Retiring completely at age sixty = 92% plan success rate
- Retiring completely at age sixty-two = 95% plan success rate
- Semi-retiring at age sixty = 96% plan success rate
- Semi-retiring at age sixty-two = 99% plan success rate

All the scenarios we ran for them already incorporated the various assumptions and optionality we had discovered on their gathering calls (e.g., hiring a tennis coach for their youngest, increasing the travel budget, allocating funds for both kids' summer camps, and, most impactfully, not assuming any further income bumps to account for the fact that they were prioritizing family time over career advancement for the next decade).

It seemed that no matter how much more stress (via additional spending or goals) we thought we were adding to their plan, the outcomes remained within the desired range. I had an epiphany while trying to explain to Jake and Stephanie just how unique their plan results were and why they were in such terrific shape: Their day-to-day spending habits could not hurt them because they had already crushed the bigger spending decisions.

I wanted to drill this point home because they were frugal by nature. I needed to show them they could genuinely increase their spending in a few areas that were important to them, with zero negative ramifications. They needed to hear this, and hearing their positive reaction (and how they looked at each other) as I shared this over our Zoom call was the highlight of my week.

I explained that any spending increase in the day-to-day decisions didn't matter (within reason) because they had already aced the big financial decisions (homes, cars, debt, income) that move the needle.

Here are a few examples:

- They bought a first home that was well within their spending capacity—only 12% of their gross income went to housing.
- They never spent hundreds of thousands of dollars remodeling the home, and they were never in a rush to buy a bigger home before they really needed to.
- They didn't buy (or lease) a nice car before they could absolutely afford it.
- They had no debt, no personal loans, and no long-term obligations working against them.
- They did not buy a rental property that ate up the bulk of their liquidity, all while the rental income barely covered the mortgage (we'll get there!).
- They never let their emergency reserve drop below a number they had determined was comfortable.

Here's the point: When you have no outstanding debt or liabilities, and when your mortgage is a manageable monthly amount (and could even be paid off if you wanted to) and you have a stable income, your financial plan cannot be negatively affected by an extra few thousand spent on a vacation, enjoying a few more nights dining out, buying Starbucks coffees, or any of the other inane spending areas that financial "gurus" seem to spend all their time focusing on.

(In fact, as an aside: The whole premise of becoming wealthy by not spending money on avocado toast and Starbucks

is dumb for a few reasons, but for people of a certain income—
$300K+—the main reason is that these costs are just too
small to make any real kind of impact!)

And it goes both ways—who cares if you choose not to
spend an extra $5K on vacation or you don't spend the $30
per week on coffee when you have a Mercedes that you pay
$1,200 per month on, you have a mortgage (and property
taxes and maintenance) that runs $12K per month and eats
up 22% of your gross income, a private school payment that
costs $50K per year, and you're taking out $200K to renovate your home!

As I'm fond of sharing with clients, and as I'll say here
again: The goal in building out your financial plan is not to get
you to cut back your spending so radically that you're sitting in
retirement at age ninety "rich" but not yet having enjoyed the
fruits of your labors. That is not successful financial planning,
despite the way financial advisors are too often characterized
in pop culture. Our goal in building out your financial plan
is simple: How do we maximize your lifestyle, experiences,
and quality of life now without negatively compromising your
ability to attain financial independence later?

A big part of striking this balance is understanding the
effects (and proportional value) of the major financial decisions you make compared to the day-to-day choices that don't
have much of an impact. In the next section, we'll look at
this divide and how it manifests in practice by discussing
two clients I've recently started working with.

10

Are You Focused on Solving the $10 Problem or the $10K Problem?

"I love money. I love everything about it. I bought some pretty good stuff. Got me a $300 pair of socks. Got a fur sink. An electric dog polisher. A gasoline powered turtleneck sweater. And, of course, I bought some dumb stuff, too."
— Steve Martin

I've recently started working with two separate clients who needed help focusing on what truly mattered (even though that's not why they initially reached out to us or what they thought they needed help with). With both clients, I explained that my job is to provide guidance and ask questions that need to be addressed if they're going to maneuver into the best financial position possible . . . even (and sometimes especially!) if those aren't the questions they initially thought were important.

A great financial planner is not an order taker or ChatGPT, spouting out facts in response to every question. A great financial planner understands when a client needs to get out of their own way and when they need to ask a different question to ultimately reach their destination.

Example One

A forty-seven-year-old client came to us very focused on the fact that the tax abatement on her rental property would disappear in the next few years. She was fixated on how this tax abatement, as well as factors such as depreciation, might impact her plan and whether she should sell the property or keep renting it out.

Meanwhile:

- She has $400K sitting in money markets/CDs that have historically barely kept up with inflation.

- She has two kids and no life insurance or disability insurance outside of employment (and even that doesn't cover 40% of what she needs).
- She has no taxable investments, so all of her investable assets are in retirement accounts that are inaccessible until age fifty-nine and a half and will one day be taxable as ordinary income.

If we spent more of our time analyzing the tax abatement and depreciation (both of which, quite frankly, "are what they are") in lieu of these fundamental issues, we would be missing the forest for an individual leaf. And even when it comes to the real estate question, it's not a simple math equation, and it's definitely not a question that the tax details alone adequately capture.

The real questions to start with on the property issue are:

1. Does she want to physically maintain the property?
2. Is the income generated worth the hassle?
3. What's the opportunity cost (in return and in time) for selling?
4. If she keeps it . . . what's the endgame?

I also find that real estate questions about selling versus keeping a property almost always boil down to personal experience, as well as how you want to spend or organize your time as you get older. It's far from just a financial equation. All the analysis in the world won't change the feeling you get (or don't get) when you get a call at 2 a.m. telling you there's a leak in the bedroom.

Example Two

A forty-five-year-old doctor came to us with a lot of thoughts and questions about investment glide paths and safe distribution rates for his money. He had a large investment portfolio and had been digging deep into the latest academic research.

Meanwhile:

- He has an (admittedly smaller) Roth IRA that has been sitting in a mix of cash and expensive fixed-income mutual funds for years, while the market has been on a phenomenal run.

- He is in excellent, all-around financial shape. Because of his spending rate, financial goals, and savings/investing rate, he is on track to achieve all his short- and long-term financial goals.

The first point, about his Roth IRA, is an error I see often. People can become obsessed with squeezing out an extra percentage point (which may or may not exist) on some big asset they watch like a hawk, when they'd get a lot more value from cleaning up a smaller account with more glaring issues.

His main concern—sequence of returns risk (i.e., protecting against market volatility when you distribute funds from your portfolio)—is important . . . but, quite frankly, it's not so important for a forty-five-year-old doctor who's looking to work at least another fifteen years, and to whom sequence of returns risk won't rear its head for at least another decade. (And even then, it's not something to "worry" about; it's just a strategy to put in place as part of his retirement income plan once we get there.) All the analysis in the world won't change that today.

The far more important point toward addressing his concerns is the following: What are we trying to accomplish by spending MORE time thinking about this? Aren't we trying to use your money to improve your life . . . and not the other way around? Sometimes my job is to let clients know when there are diminishing returns on further analysis, that they have "solved" what can be solved, and it's time to go out and enjoy the day! I genuinely mean that. If you are on track to financial independence, your net worth is growing, you've optimized your investment and tax program as much as reasonably possible, and your family is protected if something bad were to happen . . . how much time should YOU be spending analyzing your finances? Any additional "improvements" don't move the needle, and any time you spend trying is time you will never get back. Knowledge is good and making sure you're not missing anything is great . . . but you don't go to a doctor to have them show you the charts. You want the doctor to tell you what to do when you leave their office so that you don't spend another minute worrying about what doesn't matter.

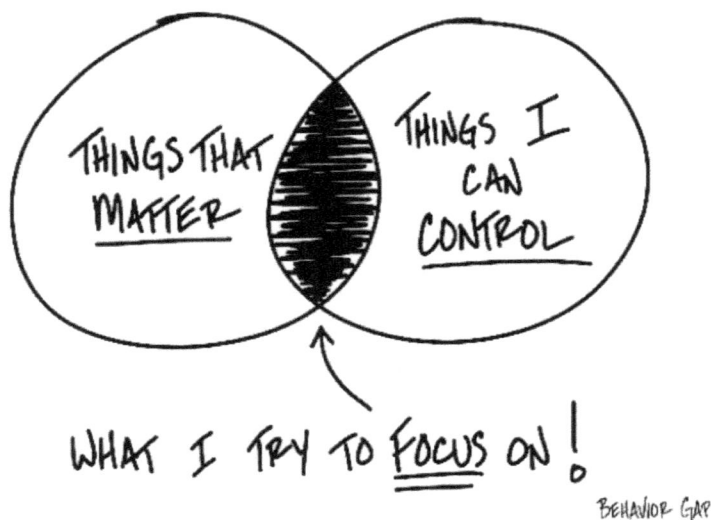

THINGS THAT MATTER

THINGS I CAN CONTROL

WHAT I TRY TO FOCUS ON!

BEHAVIOR GAP

There are plenty of advisors who will tell you what you want to hear and provide the analysis you asked for, all while knowing how little it matters. They do this not for any nefarious reason, but because they think their job is to answer your questions. It's not.

Our job is to help you take decisive action in ways that will improve your financial standing, and which you wouldn't have been able to take without us. The path to financial independence isn't paved with wishful thinking or hoping for the best. It's built on deliberate action, strategic planning, and the courage to confront what's really happening with your money.

You've now seen the fundamental challenges high earners face: the dangerous income paradox, the gap between strategy and success, and the various hurdles along the way. There's a lot to be done to get a grip on it all. But before you reach for the anxiety meds, just remember: There are tried-and-true frameworks and behaviors that work. In Part 2, I'll hand you the philosophical frameworks and tactical strategies you need to transform your financial future. You're about to discover the money philosophies that have guided hundreds of my clients from financial uncertainty to a deeper and more confident relationship with their money and their financial decision-making.

PART 2
MONEY PHILOSOPHIES TO LIVE BY

"Any intelligent fool can make things bigger, more complex, and more violent. It takes a touch of genius—and a lot of courage to move in the opposite direction."
– E.F. Schumacher

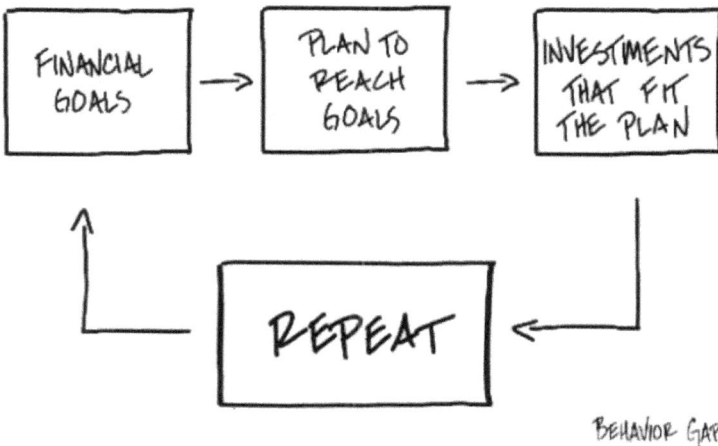

BEHAVIOR GAP

11

The Eleven Most Impactful Financial Myths

"People calculate too much and think too little."
– Charlie Munger

So, what's a money philosophy, anyway?

I'll tell you what it isn't. A money philosophy is not an academic theory or an Instagram-friendly money hack, promising you'll retire by thirty-five if you buy their course and learn how to become a real estate mogul. The philosophies I share in this book are battle-tested principles forged in the crucible of working with professionals just like you.

In fact, they are lessons gleaned from partnering with hundreds of other families just like yours. That's the beauty of working with clients in the same cohort (age, income, and stage of life): Identifiable lessons, themes, and epiphanies start to stand out!

And so, the difference between those who merely earn well and those who build lasting wealth isn't talent, luck, or even income level. It's the money philosophies you base your financial decision-making around—and a rigorous commitment to bringing them to life.

Think of them as the operating system for your financial life. You can have the best hardware (your high income), but without the right software to direct it, you'll never maximize its potential.

I've watched clients transform their financial decision-making after internalizing these concepts—from the senior product manager who finally stopped equating market volatility with risk to the mother of a growing family who realized her home wasn't the investment everyone claimed.

Fair warning: Some of the philosophies I'm about to share fly directly in the face of conventional wisdom. Your neighbor, your parents, even that obnoxious finance guy at the company holiday party might tell you I'm wrong. That's okay. These principles aren't flashy, and they will NOT get you rich overnight, but they do work—consistently and powerfully—for most folks willing to apply them.

We'll start by addressing the eleven most pervasive myths about building wealth—things my team and I discuss with clients every single day. Here's a punchy version—but don't worry, we'll unpack all these ideas at greater length as we move through the book.

1. I need seven streams of (passive) income.

This is the one I want to yell loudest about from the rooftops. The truth is: No, you *really* don't. The people I know who earn the highest incomes have spent exactly zero time focusing on novel "passive" income strategies. Instead, they have dedicated their time and energy to maximizing their primary source of income! They have learned new skills, invested in expanding their knowledge base, and utilized their brainpower and resources to become indispensable to their companies (and the industry at large), thereby continuing to earn more money each year. (And if they're a business owner, they've focused obsessively on offering a better service/product and generating additional revenue.)

If you maximize your primary source of income, and if we do our job helping you compound your wealth over decades, you will already have an asset base from which to derive future passive income. But accumulating that wealth in the first place requires a commitment to constantly increasing **one** income stream . . . not starting seven. Read more about this in Chapters 21 and 32.

2. I should take any opportunity each year to defer taxes that are available to me.

This mindset is exactly what can lead to, as planners like to call it, "the Retirement Ticking Tax Time Bomb." This is when you have all your retirement assets in pre-tax vehicles (traditional IRA, traditional 401[k], etc.) and are unknowingly setting yourself up to pay ordinary income tax on ALL this money in retirement when you start taking distributions!

For most Americans who are chiefly relying on Social Security, a small pension, and some small investment dividends in retirement, this isn't necessarily a problem, as they'll probably be in a lower tax bracket in retirement when they pay these taxes But what might be great financial advice for 99% of Americans probably isn't when it comes to tax planning for the top 1% of income earners. Simply put, if you're making $300K+ in your early forties, are compounding your wealth over decades, and are used to a certain "lifestyle," the tax equation is a bit different.

If that's you, you're probably not going to be in a "low" tax bracket at any stage of life. The future distributions from your traditional 401(k)/traditional IRA alone will be high enough to keep you in a relatively high tax bracket when you retire, and that's not even accounting for other income! It's just not our experience that high-income earners substantially lower their quality of life in retirement (nor should they), so we need to focus not just on your income needs and tax bill today, but on what they will be tomorrow!

All of which means that effective tax planning is about lowering your LIFETIME tax bill . . . not your tax bill next tax season! Read more about this in Chapters 25 and 27.

3. Buying is always better than renting, and my primary home is an investment.

Renting can afford you flexibility to change plans as your life evolves and the opportunity to invest more capital in higher-appreciating assets. It also means not paying property taxes, insurance, and maintenance fees, and it comes with an excellent ROH—return on hassle. Don't get me wrong: When the timing is right and cash flow supports it, buying a home is absolutely the right decision (most of our clients are homeowners!). It's just not ALWAYS the right decision. As a related note, when you do buy, your primary home is a place to live, NOT an investment (at least, historically, not a very good one . . . as we will get into later!). Read more about this in Chapters 19 and 21.

4. High income means future financial success.

We've discussed this point enough, so I'll just add this: Our team has done hundreds of financial plans that incorporate scenario planning. After a certain point, income is NOT one of the top three variables that drive the plan's results. (So, what *are* the top three? You already know the first one: savings rate. Then it's housing costs, followed by the cost of your future goals relative to your growth in income.) Read more about this in Chapters 4 and 5.

5. I own enough life insurance to protect my family.

If you make $500K and have people who depend on you, you should have at least $4–5M of life insurance. Term insurance can be done cost-effectively. It is always surprising to me how many people making mid-six figures will hesitate to pay $2K per year for $5M of tax-free death benefits that would cover their family's living expenses, mortgage, education costs, and health costs if they passed away prematurely. Read more about this in Chapter 22.

6. My bonus gets taxed at a higher rate than my salary.

All ordinary income is taxed at the same rate. Bonuses are often withheld at a higher rate, which lowers the amount of the bonus that gets deposited into your bank account. But your bonus, salary, and RSUs are all considered together in arriving at your marginal tax rate and your total tax liability. Unlike the other myths here, there's no action step or change in behavior to call out here, so I'll use this space to emphasize how important it is to review your tax return each year (or allow your wealth/tax team to do so) and understand what's happening under the hood! Read more about this in Chapter 25.

7. The 529 plans are too restrictive . . . what if my kids don't go to college?

Here's a (scary) fact: College costs have risen significantly faster than any other expense and have dramatically outpaced general inflation over the last thirty years. Here are some comforting facts: 529 plans can be used for K-12 private schools. You can change the beneficiary on 529 plans whenever you want, so if your oldest child doesn't use all their 529 plan for college, you can make your youngest the new beneficiary. You can also pass 529 plan balances down generationally (so if your kids don't need all the funds for whatever reason, you can get a jump start on funding your grandchildren's education). And you are allowed to roll over a portion of your unused 529 plan balance into your own Roth IRAs to help with retirement planning. And this just scratches the surface of their many benefits. That said, they are not the entire solution to education funding (and saving for your kids more broadly). We'll want to explore every tool available to us to make sure you're giving your kids the best financial start for their future. Read more about this in Chapter 29.

8. Only the super wealthy and large families need an estate plan.

Well, actually, you already have an estate plan. It's just that if *you* didn't put together your estate plan, the government did it for you. And I promise, whether you're single and childless or you have five kids, and whether you have a $200K net worth or $20M . . . that's not what you want. Read more about this in Chapter 24. Estate planning is necessary if:

1. You care about how your assets are distributed upon your demise (to family, friends, or charity).
2. You want to be in control of your own health and end-of-life planning.
3. You want to transfer your wealth in the most tax-efficient way possible.

9. I should limit my stock market investments because stocks are risky and unstable.

Since 1960, the stock market has gone up 114 times, excluding dividends. (The S&P 500, an index of the 500 largest companies in the US, was at 59.89 at the start of 1960 and, as of November 2025, it's at 6,800!) With dividends reinvested, $100K invested in 1990 (only thirty-five years ago!) would be worth more than $2.7M today. That's a 27x return. While past performance does not guarantee future results, it's fair to say that, historically, the stock market has been the greatest source of wealth expansion in human history. We confuse the stock market's very real "volatility" with its perceived "risk" at our own peril. Read more about this in Chapters 11 and 16.

Bonus corollary myth: I need to own fifteen funds to be properly diversified.[2] This is also a myth! More funds do not mean more diversification. You can accomplish the exact same level of diversification across asset classes, sectors, and styles with four to seven properly allocated, tax-efficient, low-cost funds. After this, the more funds you own, the more potential for redundancy, high operating expenses, inefficient tax treatment, and missed rebalancing. So, I guess you're getting one extra myth from me (I couldn't help myself!). Consider it a bonus for buying the book. Read more about this in Chapter 17.

10. I don't need to map out my future financial goals . . . I'll just keep making and saving more money.

Most people treat their future selves with the same intention and care that they offer strangers . . . not much. The more you outline your future financial priorities, and the more vivid those dreams are (e.g., I want to take my family on a two-week trip to Europe the year after I retire, or I want to buy a vacation home in the country when I turn sixty-two so my grandkids have a place to grow up outside the city), the more well-defined your future self becomes, and the more likely you are to change your behavior to actually benefit your future self. (Read more about this in . . . literally the whole book!)

11. I need to find that one great investing idea, that one mind-blowing tax strategy, or that one financial maneuver to become financially successful.

Attaining financial independence—meaning that you're not dependent on a paycheck to live the life you want to live—is accomplished by being disciplined, organized, and intentional with your money. There is no secret—and I would argue that anyone touting any strategy or product as the way to get wealthy is selling you something . . . and doing so transparently. Read more about this in Chapter 32.

Those are my eleven financial myths (plus one extra because once I get going, it's hard to turn it off!).

Let's end this chapter by refocusing on facts. To reach your desired future financial outcome, you'll need to:

1. Define your desired future financial outcomes.

2. Build a plan, designed with significant margin for error, that serves as your roadmap to getting there.

3. Use the plan as a working foundation and update it as your life evolves.

These myths aren't just theoretical misconceptions; they're the practical roadblocks I see preventing smart, successful professionals from achieving their financial potential every day. They represent the gap between conventional wisdom and actual financial practice.

In the following chapters, we'll systematically dismantle these myths and replace them with powerful frameworks that will transform your relationship with money. We'll start with the most fundamental shift in perspective: Investment volatility is not the same as investment risk. And more volatility does NOT equal more risk.

Let's dive deeper into why the fear of market volatility might be the single biggest threat to your financial independence—and what you can do about it.

12

Investing:
Volatility Is NOT Risk

"I never attempt to make money on the stock market. I buy on the assumption that they could close the market the next day and not reopen it for ten years."
– Warren Buffett

I'd venture to guess that many of you have completed a "risk tolerance questionnaire" once or twice in your life. This is when you answer a series of questions about your comfort level when it comes to making and losing money with your investments, and then the program (or the advisor who receives the questionnaire) spits out some type of risk number, which supposedly translates to the way you "should" be investing your life savings, forever and ever.

The way people are asked to think about and quantify their "risk tolerance" leads many potential investors to believe that their "risk number" is inherently important. It's seen as somehow central to who you are as an investor, like the financial equivalent of tracking your blood pressure during a medical checkup. The implicit idea behind these question-naires is that your resultant risk number should determine the level of risk you take on with your money. (If you earned a score of "X," then you're "moderately" aggressive and you should have the following asset allocation . . .)

To be candid, I think using a person's "risk tolerance" to determine a targeted investment allocation can be devastatingly detrimental if the goal is to make the best financial decisions for their future. In my personal experience as a CFP® working with hundreds of clients, I've found that many people complete these risk questionnaires without ever unpacking what the word "risk" really means . . . and what it doesn't.

Most of the time, risk questionnaires do not actually quantify your appetite for long-term risk. Rather, they determine your ability to stomach *short-term volatility*. That's why most of the questions ask you to react to the hypothetical scenario of losing money in the next six months.

But risk and volatility are two entirely different ideas when it comes to your investing future. And unless you truly understand the difference between the two, you could be shortchanging your financial and investing potential.

Let's break it down.

The volatility of a particular investment only measures the degree to which that investment's price might fluctuate in the short term (both up *and* down . . . though we tend to only think about volatility when investment values drop). Volatility is, therefore, a word only used to describe an investment's temporary behavior!

Knowing that an investment is "volatile" tells you absolutely nothing about whether it will be a successful investment in the long term or, even more generally, whether the price will go up or down over time. It merely tells you how much and how often you can expect the price to fluctuate along the way.

On the other hand, the *risk* of any investment is based on its likelihood of losing your money in the long run. Just think about the word "risk" as it applies to any other area in your life (e.g., a "risky" surgery or making a "risky" throw in football). A risky surgery is one with a high chance of losing the patient, and a risky throw is one with a higher-than-average chance of being dropped. In these two examples (and in all other walks of life), "risk" signifies the chance of permanent failure . . . of doing something that you can't undo, and which leaves you in a worse condition and with fewer options.

So, what does that mean when it comes to investing? In investing, failure means not having the money you need when you need it. This is the only time when price volatility turns into actual risk (i.e., losing money). If you have an investment account and it declines 20% when you're ten years away from withdrawing the funds, well, we're not talking about anything close to permanent failure (risk)— you still have years for that money to grow and earn the returns you're looking for. Assuming that you don't sell, the only place you have "lost" money, thus far, is on paper.

All of which means that investment risk, properly defined, refers to anything that increases the likelihood of a *permanent* loss of capital or the *permanent* erosion of capital (meaning your money doesn't grow as much as you need it to). These are the only two real risks we are worried about when it comes to saving and investing money, and they really boil down to the same thing: investing your money in a way that doesn't provide the return you need by the time you're ready to spend it down.

To summarize: An investment's risk is determined by the likelihood that it will be worth less at some future point when you need access to the funds, whereas volatility is determined by how much its price goes up and down along the way. Volatility is, therefore, tracked in days and months. Risk is measured in decades.

Reframing concepts like risk and volatility is important not merely as a thought exercise, but because it leads to real differences in investing outcomes! When we fill out risk tolerance questionnaires, we are unwittingly accepting their (historically inaccurate!) premise that stock market investments are "risky" and cash/fixed income are "safe."

The thinking goes like this: The way you answer the questions might indicate that you're more "aggressive," which would be interpreted to mean you should own more stock market investments, or more conservative, which would mean you should own more bonds and fixed income. This is the foundational logic of every risk questionnaire you've ever taken. But this is nonsensical because there is simply no evidence to support the argument that stocks (as an asset class) are riskier than bonds, when viewed over the appropriate amount of time you should be holding these investments for in the first place!

Capital invested in the stock market has increased ninety-seven times (!!!) over the last sixty-five years (and that excludes dividends, which have increased dramatically as well), and the stock market has averaged a *10% annual rate of return* over that time period![3]

Growth of $1 invested in the S&P 500
Since 1950

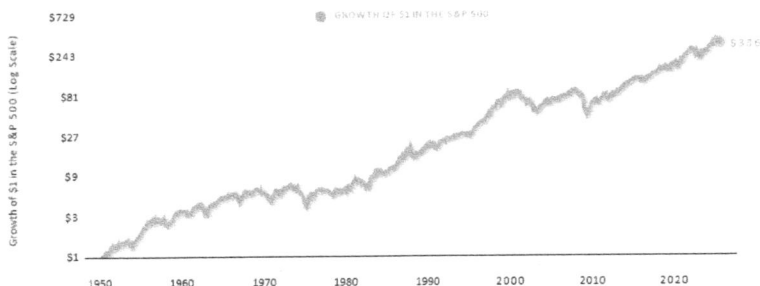

Source: © Exhibit A, FactSet Research Systems, Inc., Standard & Poor's | Latest 2025-05-01[4]

So, where did the idea that diversified stock market investing is risky come from? From people mistaking the stock market's (very real) volatility for its (historically nonexistent) long-term risk! And make no mistake, the stock market is quite volatile. Prices will fluctuate wildly—in the short term. Here are some indicators of just how volatile the stock market is:

- Stocks lose 30% of their value once every five to six years.[5]
- Within an average calendar year, you can expect the stock market to swing 14% from its high-water mark to its low point. That's a giant swing to your accounts to deal with, emotionally, every single year![6] You can see, in the chart below, the lowest point (in red) that the market reached in any given year. Again, a 14% swing was average—a lot of these were a lot lower!
- Stocks have lost half of their value three separate times since 1972.[7]

- Over a one-day period, the stock market has roughly a 50% chance of making money.[8]

S&P 500 intra-year declines vs. calendar year returns
Despite average intra-year drops of 14.1%, annual returns were positive in 34 of 45 years

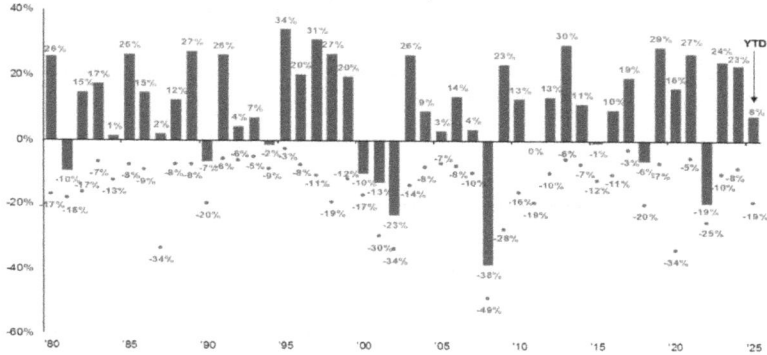

Now, if we zoom out, here are some indicators of the stock market's *risk*:

- Stocks have provided an ANNUAL 10% rate of return over the last one hundred years.[9]
- Every single twenty-year period in the history of the stock market has had positive returns.[10] (You can see this visually on the next graph we share.)
- The dividend rate of the S&P 500 has grown at a faster rate than inflation over the last seventy-five years.[11] That is to say that the dividends your investments generated, even without all that capital appreciation, would have provided enough income to offset rising prices!

Simply put, volatility is, in fact, NOT the same thing as risk. Enduring the short-term market swings endemic to stocks will lead to the greater returns you get by relentlessly owning the same stocks through it all. As an equity (stock market) investor, you are literally being compensated (in the form of higher returns) to stomach those short-term price fluctuations. The trade-off of living with short-term uncertainty as a stock market investor is the historical reality that you will benefit from greater long-term gains.

And in case you need even more evidence:

- Stocks are up twelve times since 1990, stock dividends are up five times, and inflation is only up two times.[12] (I repeat the fact about dividends versus inflation because, even for the retired investor who needs her income to grow faster than her costs, stocks are incredibly valuable and productive . . . but I digress!)

- The longest it has ever taken an investor to recover an original investment in the stock market (including reinvested dividends) was the five-year, eight-month period from August 2000 through April 2006.[13]

Reread the volatility and risk metrics, back-to-back (c'mon, it's the previous page!).

The second set of facts literally makes the first set irrelevant! That's to say that there has not been a single market correction in history from which you would have benefited by selling out of your diversified equity positions (as the chart below confirms!). In fact, selling is literally the only way you can turn a temporary market decline into a permanent loss . . . which means that the stock market itself has never actually lost money. Only human beings are uniquely capable of turning a temporary decline in the stock market into a permanent loss.

How Often S&P 500 Was Higher Over Various Holding Periods
Since 1950

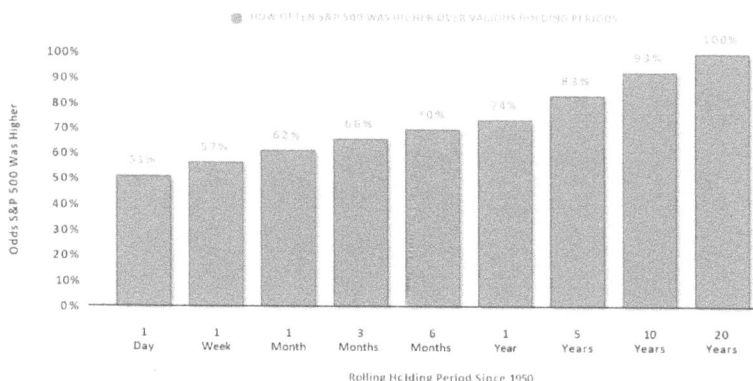

Source: © Exhibit A, FactSet Research Systems, Inc., Standard & Poor's | Latest 2025-05-01

Ladies and gentlemen, this should drive us all crazy. The greatest possible way to compound your wealth and fund your long-term goals (the stock market) is considered "risky" because its frequent price fluctuations, or volatility, are being mistaken for actual, real-world loss.

This mistaken assumption has an even more infuriating compounding effect: In the average investor's quest to lower or limit volatility (by decreasing equity exposure), they are, by default, also lowering the historical long-term returns of their portfolio. While stocks have earned an annualized 10% return over the last century, bonds have only earned approximately 4%.[14] (To be fair to bonds—this number feels a bit exaggerated right now because bonds are having such a terrible decade through 2025, but even if you exclude the 2020s, bonds have only earned 6% as compared to the stock market's 10%.)

But the real (as opposed to nominal) difference between asset classes is actually bigger than that! If we subtract 3% inflation from the mix (because we only care how much our money has grown relative to the cost of living), stocks have earned 7% annually and bonds have earned slightly less than 1.5%. And, again, even if we subtract the current decade's terrible bond performance (thus far), the difference, net of inflation, is still significant: 7% average return for owning stocks compared to 3% return for owning bonds. That's a *drastic* difference in investment outcome! Stock investors were able to compound their net-of-inflation investment at more than twice the rate the bondholder received.

It's worth highlighting how stocks and bonds have faired over the last thirty years (see chart on following page). The more interesting point to make here is that these differences in returns are both natural, obvious, and structural once we think about what it is we're doing when we invest in stocks and bonds!

Deciding whether to own stocks or bonds is to ask yourself a simple question: Do you want to own shares of companies (stock investing) or do you want to lend money to those same companies (bond investing) in return for interest payments?

Once you realize this is what you're doing, it's merely common sense that the owners of great companies must

Change in purchasing power by investment in major asset class
Growth of $10,000, adjusted for inflation, from 1994-2024, annual returns

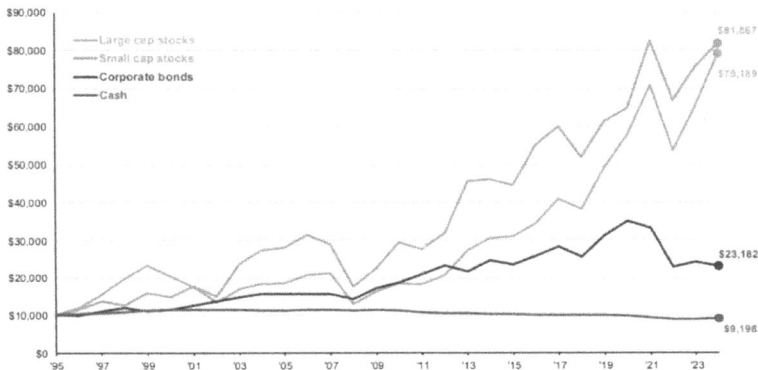

Source: Bloomberg, Bureau of Labor Statistics, Ibbotson, J.P. Morgan Asset Management.
Large cap stocks: IA SBBI Large Cap TR Index; Small cap stocks: IA SBBI Small Cap TR Index; Corporate bonds: Bloomberg Long U.S. Corporate Index; Cash: IA SBBI T-bill Index. All returns are inflation-adjusted total returns, using annual average headline CPI inflation.
Guide to the Markets – U.S. Data are as of August 8, 2025.

earn a return far greater than the interest they pay to lenders, or they wouldn't borrow money in the first place! In other words, when a company issues bonds to the public, they're asking you to lend it money and, in return, the company will pay you interest while you hold their bonds. Think about it: The company issuing the bonds would NEVER do this without being absolutely convinced it can take your money and reinvest it in a way that will lead to greater returns compared to the interest they have to pay back to you!

Once we add that basic framing, we can more readily internalize the fact that the *owners* of great companies have always been paid substantially more than the *lenders* to those great companies ever did or ever could.

And naturally, by owning bonds and reducing their expected return, these investors have (knowingly or unknowingly) decreased the probability of attaining their financial goals—because if their investments grow at a slower rate, they will have less money to afford those goals! In other words, they are creating *more* risk (meaning, more likelihood of not having enough money when they need it) by trying to avoid another risk (permanent stock market failure) that, historically, has never come to pass.

Understanding that volatility and risk are fundamentally different concepts transforms the way we approach investing. True risk isn't about day-to-day price fluctuations—it's about the permanent loss of capital and the possibility of outliving your money (and one leads to the other).

So now that THAT's out of the way, let's explore another commonly misunderstood investing principle: the difference between your risk tolerance and your risk capacity. As we'll see, these two concepts are often conflated by both investors and financial planners, leading to investment strategies that may feel comfortable but will undermine your long-term financial goals.

13

Investing: Risk Tolerance vs. Risk Capacity

"The big money is not in the buying or the selling, but in the waiting."
— Charlie Munger

On a recent phone call, a prospective client told me that her previous advisor had asked her to fill out a risk tolerance questionnaire, and because the software deemed her "conservative," she hadn't been investing in the stock market. At all. I almost fell out of my chair. Not because she should or should not be investing in the stock market. That's not the point here. It's the idea of financial advisors relying solely on software-generated risk tolerance questionnaires that is BAFFLING to me.

This person was a physician, so here's how I put it to her: Imagine going to the doctor and having the doctor choose a medicine or remedy based on your WebMD search history, rather than running tests, asking deeper questions, or gauging family history. What's the point of going to an expert if that expert is just going to rely on the misconceptions, half-truths, and Wikipedia answers that you already had when you came into the appointment?

Let's peel this back.

Risk "tolerance" refers to how much risk you are emotionally comfortable taking on in your portfolio. It is not about your financial circumstances or reality . . . it's just how you feel about investing. Your risk tolerance is therefore totally dependent on your knowledge and general investing awareness, and can be advanced through education, better planning, and a greater awareness of investing principles.

In my experience, most people have a risk "tolerance" that is entirely surface-level and ready to be changed. Risk "tolerance" is paper-thin. Clients who have told me they're "conservative" on an initial call have realized by the end of the conversation that they just didn't really understand stock market investing. They assumed it involved day trading individual stocks, when in fact, it can mean owning a globally diversified index fund that owns the entire market at once. This is a simple example, but it helps show that words like "aggressive" and "conservative" mean entirely different things to different people.

Instead of risk "tolerance," I prefer to focus on risk *capacity*. Risk capacity refers to how much you can truly stand to lose, based on your cash flow, your liquidity, your upcoming big-ticket expenses, and your income. Risk capacity should dictate how you invest—and you can only know your risk capacity through proper planning.

For example, if you have $100K in the bank and we determine that your six-month cash cushion is $50K, your upcoming house renovation will cost $25K, and we want to leave some room to cover potential tax liability . . . well, guess what? You have ZERO risk capacity with this bucket of money. It should all be set aside in cash or cash alternatives: high-yield savings, money markets, CDs, and so on. You cannot afford to risk losing this money, because you need it soon to pay for confirmed costs.

Alternatively, if you are forty-five years old, have $900K in your 401(k), make $500K, own your own home, and have ample liquidity . . . you can stand to handle quite a bit of volatility in the short term, understanding that you don't need access to these funds for fifteen-plus years. Your risk capacity is substantially higher than a risk tolerance questionnaire might lead you to believe by asking you questions about how you feel, in the abstract.

This might be a good time to briefly mention my attitude toward Bitcoin (because you won't find it elsewhere in the book!). My views here are quite boring: I don't think it's the panacea that the Bitcoin zealots believe and I don't take a hard "absolutely not" position that so many advisors still seem to. For an investor with a high-risk capacity and a high-risk tolerance (in this case, I would say both matter because there's relatively little history available), I think it could make sense to allocate 2–5% of your portfolio to the asset class as a diversification strategy.

Now, of course, losing money—even if it's temporary and even if you DO have a genuinely high *risk capacity*—is never fun. In fact, it can be downright terrifying. But it's frustrating beyond belief that the financial media seems committed to and, in fact, even obsessed with beating you over the head with the stock market's day-to-day prices, even though these have never, ultimately, mattered.

When we laser in on understanding your risk capacity, we realize that those price swings should have absolutely zero bearing on your decades-long investment program.

I, for one, can't understand why I'm supposed to care about an investment's short-term price swings instead of its potential for making me more money than other asset classes in the long run. If I'm investing my money, it's because I don't need it right now and have no intention of selling for at least five, and more likely ten-plus, years. So, of course, I would prefer a "bumpy" 7% return over a smooth 3% return over the next thirty years. It will mean I have more money at the end of the day, and that's the entire point of deferring capital and investing!

If I'm investing my IRA for another thirty years, and I know (based on all available history) that I will maximize the size of that account at age sixty-two by investing entirely in diversified mainstream equities instead of bonds, WHY WOULD I POSSIBLY CARE that it might go down temporarily when I'm thirty-three, thirty-seven, and forty-five? I'm not investing the money to take it out when I'm thirty-three or forty-five. The goal is to maximize money when you need it . . . not to maximize the price when you don't.

I'll conclude with this: My role as financial planner and wealth advisor is to put my clients in the best possible position to reach their long-term financial goals. This often involves making choices that may not be comfortable in the near term. My job is to educate and coach them into seeing the bigger picture and doing what needs to be done—like a personal trainer who motivates you to do those last thirty seconds of crunches because it's what you need in the end.

If I'm only there to take orders based on their comfort level or "risk capacity," why hire me at all? And if I were to let my clients' "risk tolerance" dictate how I design their portfolios, even when that strategy may not ultimately serve them best, well . . . then I should find something else to do.

Moral of the story? Risk "tolerance" is nothing but a starting point to understanding someone's preconceived notions around investing.

Now that we understand how risk tolerance differs from risk capacity, let's follow that rippling current into an eddy that may surprise you: the decision of whether to pick individual stocks.

14

Investing: Why I Don't Pick Individual Stocks

"Don't look for the needle in the haystack. Just buy the haystack!"
– John Bogle

Prospective clients, or acquaintances who've just learned what I do, often ask me if I pick my own individual stocks—assuming that as a wealth advisor, I must. They're always shocked by my answer: "Nope! It doesn't interest me, and frankly, it seems like a giant waste of time." Hence, this is a short chapter. Across all my investments, I don't have a single portfolio where I choose my own stocks.

In my experience, there are three levels of "stock and investment" knowledge:

1. "I know nothing about the stock market, so I'm going to stick to investing mostly in index funds."

2. "I've started learning about the stock market, so I'm going to start managing my own money, picking styles/sectors of the market, and choosing my own stocks."

3. "I now know enough to know that I don't know anything and cannot predict future performance, so I'm going to stick to investing mostly in index funds."

What's the beauty of choosing door three? It shows an appreciation of the levers that drive wealth creation, and a recognition that some activities are more like spinning in our chairs than creating wealth. I know that, historically, investing in a broad, diversified portfolio of stock market index funds will provide me with the rate of return I need to compound my wealth, outpace inflation, and fund my future goals. Here are some facts from a 2024 study based on the last century of stock investing:

- 52% of stocks lost money.
- 69% of stocks underperform.
- 4% of stocks accounted for nearly ALL of the gains.[15]

Friend, what are we doing here? Do we really think we are going to successfully find the needle in the haystack (i.e., the tiny fraction of companies that outperform the market over an investing lifetime)?

Here's another exercise: Look at the top ten companies (by market cap) in the S&P 500 right now and then compare that to the top ten thirty years ago, in 1995.

Here . . . we did it for you:

1995 Top S&P 500 Companies	2025 Top S & P 500 Companies
1. Exxon Mobil	1. Nvidia Corporation
2. Coca-Cola	2. Microsoft Corporation
3. General Electric (GE)	3. Apple Inc.
4. Merck & Co	4. Alphabet Inc. (Google)
5. Proctor & Gamble	5. Amazon
6. Johnson & Johnson	6. Meta Platforms (Facebook)
7. Microsoft Corporation	7. Broadcom Inc.
8. Walmart	8. Tesla Inc.
9. IBM Corporation	9. Berkshire Hathaway
10. Intel Corporation	10. JP Morgan Chase & Co

Only ONE company overlaps, and these lists are only thirty years apart! What's the takeaway? Even today's biggest, most successful companies—companies that seem to run the world—will be replaced by the unicorns of their time, just as has happened in every generation prior. Imagining that we're capable of picking only the "winners" of the next thirty years (many of which don't exist yet) is an illusion!

I'll repeat myself for emphasis: I have *never* been interested in picking my own stocks . . . not even in a "play" or "side" account. Across all my investments, I don't have a single portfolio where I choose my own stocks. It doesn't interest me, and I can't think of a worse use of my time! Let's stop obsessing over the day-to-day price fluctuations of various companies and sectors, and instead let's own the market, rebalance tax-efficiently, and let the market do what it has done remarkably well for more than two centuries: create long term wealth that we can tap into much later in life.

To that end, one of my favorite investing factoids—from the often cited Brinson, Hood, and Beebower Study (1986)—is that over 90% of your investment success is attributable to your asset allocation.[16] In other words, just picking the proper ratio between stocks and bonds is worth almost ten times more than the selection of the individual stocks and bonds themselves. The greatest investing minds in history (e.g., Warren Buffett, Peter Lynch, Franklin Templeton, Charlie Munger, and Howard Marks) are all united in their understanding that nobody can predict the stock market and that there is no "secret" to outperformance. (If there was, there would only be one fund, and we'd all have our money in it!)

All of this means, ironically perhaps, that investment selection (not the management!) is the easier part of what we do. We don't need to seek out over-performance, because the market has, historically, rewarded us just for existing. (We understand, of course, that all investments involve risk and there are no guarantees when investing!) That said, the fact that we're not picking individual stocks or expensive, actively managed funds doesn't mean you can afford to put your investments on autopilot, or that delegating investment management to a professional team isn't incredibly valuable. Even while we're focused on utilizing the market instead of trying to beat it, we are looking to improve investor outcomes through the following tax strategies and daily monitoring:

1. **Asset Location:** This means allocating your individual holdings (stocks, bonds, ETFs, mutual funds, etc.) into the most advantageous account type (taxable, pre-tax, Roth, after-tax) to minimize taxes. A few examples: We'd look to place any fixed income (which pays interest that would be taxed if it were in a brokerage account) in a pre-tax account that defers taxes year-to-year. We might place the assets with the highest expected return (small cap stocks, growth stocks, etc.) in a Roth IRA, because it grows tax-free, and we don't want to pay taxes on our highest performing positions (and because there are no RMDs, we don't have to worry about sequence of returns risk!). We might put securities with high turnover potential into a pre-tax account to avoid annual taxes, while individual stocks utilized through

a direct indexing approach designed to harvest tax losses naturally make sense in a taxable account.

2. **Rebalancing:** Rebalancing is simply the process of adjusting your portfolio back to its target allocation whenever it drifts too far from your initial intended target. So, to use a simple example, if you wanted 75% US stocks and 25% international stocks, and the market moved so that US stocks made up 85% of your portfolio, we would rebalance to bring it back to 75%! This would mean selling the asset in the portfolio that just did well (US stocks) and buying the part of the portfolio that is now underweight (international stocks) to reestablish our target. Rebalancing means, almost by definition, buying low and selling high! This can also be a helpful strategy because when any security goes up or down too much relative to its expected return—which happens when holdings in a portfolio drift from their target allocation—they are more likely to "snap back" and revert to their expected average return. Put another way, if US stocks are doing significantly better than international stocks, such that they end up becoming a larger and larger part of the portfolio, we're actually getting closer to US stocks being overvalued and their returns coming back down to Earth. That's a very broad-strokes explanation, but I hope it shows

how rebalancing based on a portfolio's "drift" allows us to take advantage of this sort of price movement over time.

3. **Tax Loss Harvesting, Custom Indexing, and Using Covered Calls on Concentrated Stock:** We'll cover this in Part 3 . . . stay tuned!

So, if we take the last few chapters together, we arrive at the following foundation:

- Historically, owning a large and globally diversified collection of the world's most profitable companies has returned about 7% annually after inflation.[17]
- A tiny subset of these companies is responsible for the majority of these gains.[18]
- The companies that are responsible for the gains change from generation to generation.
- In trying to "pick" which companies will outperform, you are statistically (and historically) MUCH, MUCH more likely to lose money than you are to outperform the market as a whole.

Because investing in the stock market is a means to an end (i.e., greater wealth), I view these facts with glee. The stock market being efficient* is a wonderful thing. It means I don't have to take excessive risk (or spend unnecessary time) trying to squeeze out a few extra percentage points (but more likely erasing most of my gains) when simply existing in the market will allow me to share in the profits of the most successful, innovative, and adaptable businesses in the world.

(*I debated spending a few pages here discussing modern portfolio theory, the capital asset pricing model, and efficient market frontiers . . . which, taken together, form the core of my firm's evidence-based investment approach.

Ultimately, however, this book is about financial decision-making, not understanding theory for the sake of theory, and these last few chapters give you all the outcomes and takeaways you need—without the fancy academic jargon!)

15

Investing: Inflation Is the Silent Killer

*"If you think the market is too high, wait
'til you see it 20 years from now."*
— Nick Murray

We've now established that passive investing outperforms stock picking for most of us mere mortals.[19] But even once you have a tax-efficient, diversified investment strategy in place, there's another threat to your financial outcomes lurking in the shadows—one that doesn't (usually) make dramatic headlines, but which quietly erodes your wealth a little, year by year.

One of the most foundational concepts for forty-year-old investors to understand is what we discussed in Chapter 11: Risk and volatility are not the same thing. In fact, though they're often mistaken for one another, getting them mixed up can lead to painful underperformance over time.

Now we need to add this next foundational concept: Money and currency are not the same thing . . . and confusing the two can be equally damaging for clients in their fifties and sixties as they approach retirement.

(To be sure, mistaking money for currency is equally damaging if you're in your thirties and forties, but it's something we see more frequently with people already at traditional retirement age. Nevertheless, because we are all planning to reach our sixties, and because I don't plan on writing a third book anytime soon, I think its well worth exploring this reality here.)

Why? Because money does not simply equate to the number of dollars that you have in your bank account, wallet, or 401(k). Money, once properly defined, means purchasing power . . . or *"How many goods and services can I buy with what I have?"* And, just like that carton of milk you forgot in the back of your refrigerator, your purchasing power has an expiration date.

How do I know this?

Well, according to the US Bureau of Labor Statistics, average inflation has been about 3% over the last fifty years. So, if you had $1M in your bank account in 1995, and you had "managed" to still have $1M in your account today, you would only be able to buy 40% of what you could have thirty years ago with the same dollar amount! Put more simply, you have lost $600K (!!!) of your "money," despite having the exact same number of dollars (since it still shows $1M in your account!).

Read that back again . . . it's crucial. Does it matter that you still have $1M on "paper" if that money can only support or generate 40% of what it could once have bought you? I think not! You have "lost" money over time, without your dollar value dropping, and without even realizing it.

Erosion From Inflation of the Purchasing Power of $10
Since July, 1983

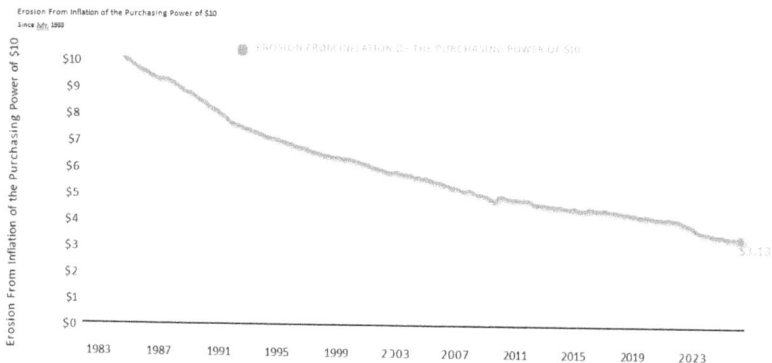

And there's the rub.

Retirement is not, chiefly, about the preservation of capital. In fact, being primarily focused on preserving your currency units (dollars) as you approach retirement age can be the surest way of ensuring that you will *run out of money* later on in retirement. Again, we have to understand that the only proper definition of "money" is purchasing power, and that focusing on preserving your "account value" will lead to inflation ravaging that purchasing power over time.

Why did I use thirty years in my example? Well, the average sixty-five-year-old, non-smoking couple today must plan for their money to last for a thirty-plus-year retirement.[20] That's right: There's a good chance one member of the couple will be alive in their nineties![21] (And if you're in your forties today, these numbers obviously look even better!)

So, the question needs to be asked: **Why do we treat people approaching retirement as if they only need to preserve their "money" for a few years?** Statistically speaking, they should plan to make their money *last* for THE NEXT THIRTY YEARS!

Their investment strategy and retirement distribution strategy should be cognizant of this reality. In my opinion and experience, utilizing only short-term vehicles that limit volatility and suppress growth (which is what we really mean when we say "preserving capital") is not a rational thirty-year plan. It can be a recipe to run out of money in the later stages of your retirement. (Of course, short-term reserves have their place in retirement, but once you've established your cash cushion, there is a point of diminishing returns.)

Common financial wisdom treats sixty-five-year-olds (and their investing needs) as if they were already ninety. And even if you're ninety years old . . . are you focused on leaving a legacy for your family? Do you think about generational planning? Because if so, a ninety-year-old who is largely investing for her family, charities, and passions is still investing for decades to come.

Instead of a focus on preserving capital, retirement is fundamentally about:

1. Outpacing inflation each decade in retirement (i.e., growing your investments).

2. Generating stable and increasing income throughout retirement (i.e., growing your income).

If you do not have a retirement strategy that is driven by the fundamental need to outpace inflation throughout this thirty-plus-year period, you may need to rethink your retirement strategy. The bottom line is that you haven't yet built out a program designed to make your money last longer than you do. (This is why I often pick on target-date funds. These funds become more conservative as you approach retirement, meaning that the appropriately balanced and diversified portfolio of equities that allowed you to grow your money through your forties and fifties automatically turns into a low-growth portfolio of fixed income and cash—and this can actually hinder your ability to live through the next thirty years of retirement.)

As you explore your own retirement planning—and maybe even as you start to become more aware of or involved in how your parents are doing things—here are the questions to ask yourself:

1. Am I limiting my ability to outpace inflation by following conventional wisdom that knows nothing of my financial means?

2. Where will my retirement income come from? (Which accounts should I pull from?)

3. Will it be enough to retire on? (How much do I need?)

4. Are my assets (and the income they generate) designed to fund and maximize a (potentially) thirty-year retirement?

5. Do I have a plan to protect against sequence of returns risk? (We are not going to delve into this concept here because it doesn't generally impact mid-career professionals—but I have to at least mention it as an important retirement consideration, or I'd feel like I was dropping the ball.)

Now that we understand inflation's sneaky wealth-eroding powers, let's talk about something that tends to cause much more immediate panic: watching your portfolio take a nosedive. Few things make investors second-guess their strategy faster than seeing their account drop by 20% in a month. As Mike Tyson said, "Everyone has a plan until they get punched in the mouth." There's no degree of intellectual "know-how" that can totally prepare us for the (natural!) feelings of anxiety and frustration that happen when we see our accounts drop. Here's the thing, though: Short-term dips don't mean your long-term goals are toast. In fact, they often open the door to opportunities most investors overlook—if you can resist the urge to panic and instead remember that volatility is just part of the ride.

16

Investing: What Do Declining Stock Prices Mean for You?

"If you're not willing to react with equanimity to a market price decline of 50% . . . you are not fit to be a common shareholder and you deserve the mediocre result you're going to get."
– Charlie Munger

Even if you have internalized everything we've been discussing, there is nothing like that feeling when you see that you've lost 20% of your portfolio value in the blink of an eye. It's worth reflecting on that moment for a minute. How did you feel as it was happening? What was going through your mind as the market went down, seemingly without rhyme or reason? It's okay to admit that it probably felt super demoralizing.

It is BRUTAL to look at your statements when it feels like all the money you've been saving for years is gone in an instant. Again, at that moment, it doesn't matter what you know to be true intellectually—and I can say that conclusively from working with clients. There is nothing like logging on and seeing your net worth substantially diminished compared to a week prior.

All of this is true. *And*, to return to the left side of your brain: Think back to the moment, post market-drop, when your accounts rebounded and ended up higher than they were before the crash (meaning you made it all back). Depending on the correction that came to mind, this might have taken thirty days, six months, or a few years!

Now think back again to the moment when your accounts were at their nadir. What did those lower retirement account balances (whether they were "down" for one month or two years) mean for you? How did these losses, which only ever existed on a piece of paper, translate to your day-to-day cash flow or your progress along your financial roadmap?

Again, and it bears repeating because I never want to come off as "that advisor": I hope you know that I'm not trying to minimize the frustration you felt at the time. I'm merely trying to get us all to think about the bigger picture. If we've done the right planning, and we have our emergency and short-term reserves properly funded, while placing our long-term money in "buckets" to maximize growth . . . well then, we won't need to pull money out to live on. And so, the only reason that declining stock prices should cause us to worry or change our approach would be if we thought this was the start of a permanent market decline in which the markets would never again reach new heights. After all, we don't freak out every winter and take the cold weather as a sign that we'll never see the summer sun again.

Every single market decline of 25% or greater (like the one we experienced in 2022, which lasted the entire year, or in April of 2025, which lasted barely a month) resulted in positive returns a mere three years later (and all but one,

When the S&P 500 is Down 25% or Worse Since 1950

Peak	Trough	% Decline	+1 Year	+3 Years	+5 Years	+10 Years
12/12/1961	6/26/1962	-28.0%	31.2%	69.2%	94.8%	171.1%
11/29/1968	5/26/1970	-36.1%	32.2%	44.3%	27.9%	97.5%
1/11/1973	10/3/1974	-48.2%	1.4%	23.8%	42.0%	188.4%
11/28/1980	8/12/1982	-27.1%	43.9%	81.2%	238.6%	403.9%
8/25/1987	12/4/1987	-33.5%	14.7%	34.1%	96.8%	387.1%
3/24/2000	10/9/2002	-49.1%	0.2%	1.9%	21.5%	38.3%
10/9/2007	3/9/2009	-56.8%	-6.9%	3.7%	61.2%	209.6%
2/19/2020	3/23/2020	-33.9%	56.4%	???	???	???
1/3/2022	9/30/2022	-25.2%	???	???	???	???
Averages		**-37.6%**	**21.6%**	**36.9%**	**83.3%**	**213.7%**

Data: Ycharts

129

a single year later!). And *five* years after the bottom? The returns were exceptional . . . every single time.

This should remind us of what we already know and have discussed in this book: Stock market declines are temporary, and their inevitable advances have been, to this point in time at least, permanent. More to the point, there has not been a single market correction in history from which you would have benefited by selling out of your equity positions. (Look at this chart for how devastating doing so would have been in 2008 and 2009 . . . your net worth would never have recovered.)

The Value of Staying Invested

Holding the S&P 500 vs Cash, Initial $100,000 Investment, Total Returns

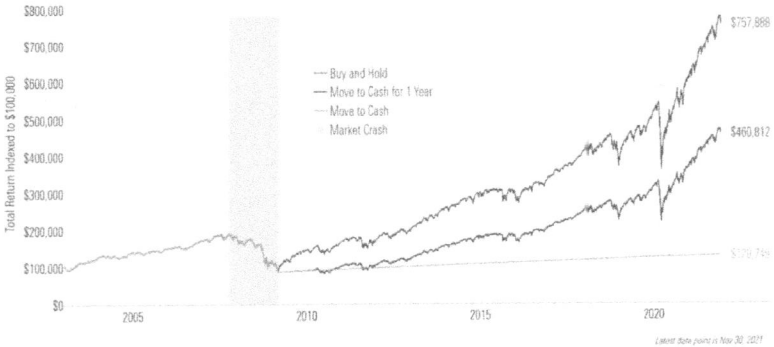

In fact, as mentioned in Chapter 11, selling is literally the only way you can turn a temporary decline into a permanent loss. I'll repeat what I said before, because it's an important point: This means that the stock market itself has never

actually lost money—only human behavior can push that particular lever.

I'll take it one step further: It's normal to worry that, as the decline gets worse and we suddenly go from 15% down to 25% down, the risk is rising, right? That everything is coming apart at the seams?

It's the opposite: your risk has diminished! You're now that much closer to the market bottom and, as logic dictates, that much closer to the inevitable market rebound, when everything starts to come back. Starting to panic now would be like running twenty-four miles of a marathon and then worrying that you might not finish. You've already put in the work and endured most of the pain . . . with each step forward, even though it's uncomfortable, you're that much closer to the end!

This is not to say that the stock market can't go down by more than 25%, or that we won't see 30% or even 40% losses. It's possible, and it's happened. It's to say that with each passing day, we are getting closer to the stock market rebounding and to us being rewarded for our patience, discipline, and steadfastness. After all, market volatility simply transfers risk from those who can't handle it to those who can.

We won't ever know when a rebound will happen, but we do know that the only real long-term investment risk you face is not being invested when it does.

And with that, I'm going to make a confession: Every time I write the words "the stock market" or "the market" or

Returns of the S&P 500
Performance of a $10,000 investment between July 1, 2005 and June 30, 2025

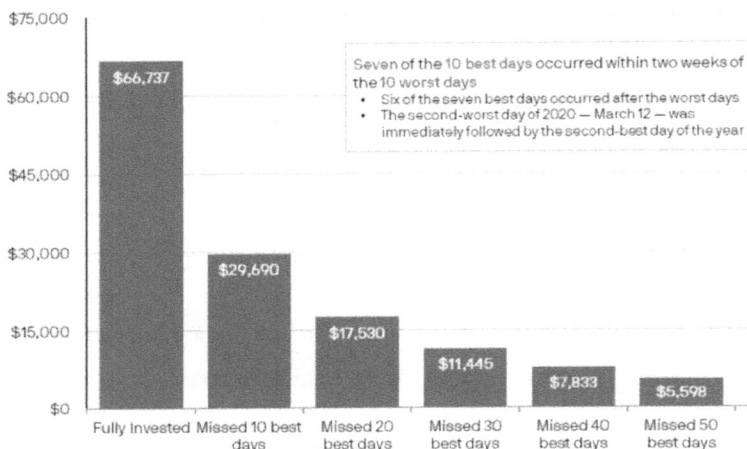

Seven of the 10 best days occurred within two weeks of the 10 worst days
- Six of the seven best days occurred after the worst days
- The second-worst day of 2020 — March 12 — was immediately followed by the second-best day of the year

Category	Value
Fully Invested	$66,737
Missed 10 best days	$29,690
Missed 20 best days	$17,530
Missed 30 best days	$11,445
Missed 40 best days	$7,833
Missed 50 best days	$5,598

Source J.P. Morgan Asset Management using data from Bloomberg.

"stock prices," I feel a bit guilty that I am adding to an unfortunately ubiquitous misconception. Because these words blind us to what we are really doing. We are not buying stocks. We are investing in companies. We do not simply own "stocks" whose prices are temporarily lower. We are stakeholders in a collection of the world's most successful businesses.

And when stock prices are down, the greatest companies in the world are being offered to us at an incredible discount. The further down these prices go, the more attractive long-term ownership of these companies becomes from a value perspective. And this gets to the heart of the matter.

I'll let Warren Buffett drive this point home. He wrote these words in one of his chairman's letters to shareholders during a 1997 market decline, and they still ring true today:

"If you expect to be a net saver during the next five years, should you hope for a higher or lower stock market during that period? Many investors get this one wrong. Even though they are going to be net buyers of stocks for many years to come, they are elated when stock prices rise and depressed when they fall. This reaction makes no sense. Only those who will be sellers of equities in the near future should be happy at seeing stocks rise. Prospective purchasers should much prefer sinking prices."

So, change your perspective! He continues:

"So smile when you read a headline that says, 'Investors lose as market falls.' Edit in your mind to, 'Disinvestors lose as market falls—but investors gain.'"

As a nice summation of his message, the stock market has suffered two of the ever market meltdowns since Mr. Buffett wrote this note—in 2000 and 2008—and neither of them matters much to the average equity investor, who has quadrupled their money over that same time period![22]

All of this should be taken to mean that the risk to you is not getting caught in a decline, however big that decline is (even if it's 20% or 30%). The risk is that by not investing at all out of fear of that decline, you will get caught out of the next 100% advance, an eventuality that your retirement plan can never survive. So, the next time you see your portfolio taking a hit and that knot forms in your stomach, try to reframe your thinking.

Those declining numbers on your statement aren't a signal to run for the hills—they're a neon sign flashing "EQUITIES ON SALE" to all who care to look. And while none of us is Warren Buffett, we can all adopt his long-term perspective. Your financial independence journey isn't a sprint to beat the market this quarter—it's a marathon where consistency and patience will win the race.

If you have built a well-developed financial plan, are making purpose-driven investment decisions, and have a solid grasp on your financial priorities:

1. Your money is specifically positioned to achieve your short, medium, and long-term financial goals.
2. You have successfully made short-term market fluctuations wholly irrelevant to your reality.

Now that we've tackled the emotional rollercoaster of market declines, let's talk about how a diverse portfolio helps you weather those storms while still capturing long-term growth. I've seen too many smart professionals think they're "diversified" because they own twelve different tech stocks. Spoiler alert: That's like saying you have a diverse diet because you eat twelve different kinds of pasta.

17

Investing: Diversification and Asset Allocation

"Investing isn't about beating others at their game. It's about controlling yourself at your own game."

– Benjamin Graham

To summarize the last few chapters: The ratio of stocks (equities) to bonds (fixed income) you own will determine your long-term investment return to a substantially greater degree than the specific funds that you pick. (By the same token, your proportion of stocks to bonds will impact the short-term price fluctuation more than the individual funds you own . . . just in the opposite direction!)

A natural and fair follow-up question might be, "Okay, Gideon, I grant you all that . . . but should we really be investing most of our money in ANY one strategy?"

Great question. My answer is twofold:

1. Yes!
2. It's not "one" strategy.

Let's take each answer in turn.

Investing in the capital (stock) markets has, historically, been the greatest way to compound your wealth and outpace inflation over time.

And so, if our goal as investors is to maximize long-term returns and give ourselves the best chance of reaching our financial goals ten, twenty, even thirty years from now, then the preponderance of our liquid net worth should be held in mainstream public equities.

Let's continue the thought. If the stock market is a better way to maximize long-term return than the other asset classes available to us (e.g., cash, fixed income, T-bills, real estate, and gold), well then, how does moving money out of equities for the sake of "diversification" make any sense? Why would we diversify ourselves into a less productive situation? That's like saying that after getting in shape by sleeping eight hours, eating healthy, and going for daily walks, you want to diversify your habits by snacking late at night.

Diversification is meant to minimize risk . . . it's not meant to minimize return!

Now to the second part of my answer: You are already plenty diversified, because within your stock market-driven portfolio, you own all sorts of companies: large-cap, small-cap, mid-cap, growth, value, dividend payers, emerging markets, and developed markets (to say nothing of the individual sectors that make up these larger categories).

Building portfolios in which we own shares in thousands of companies simultaneously is how we stay diversified while giving ourselves the greatest chance for long-term investment success. We are not relying on any one company, market sector, geographic locale, or any other narrow factor that might lead us astray. We are choosing to own ALL of it, and as I've repeated ad nauseam, the stock market as an asset class has never permanently lost money!

Too often, people make the mistake of assuming they need to own suboptimal assets purely for the sake of diversification . . . as if asset allocation and diversification were the same thing! They are not. "Asset allocation" refers to the act of investing in different categories of investments, each being its own "asset" category (e.g., bonds, cash, and real estate). An asset allocation-driven portfolio might mean having 60% in stocks, 30% in bonds, and 10% in cash. "Diversification" means not being too concentrated on any one specific strategy, in a way that increases your risk of failure if your investing thesis is wrong. (As Nick Murray likes to say, "Diversification means not having enough in any one position to get killed by it or to make a killing from it.") If, based on the way you are investing, you could be "wrong" or "right" (e.g., "I was right about investing in health care!"), and that will dictate your account's overall performance—you're not diversified. When you own the entire stock market, you might be up or down at any given point, but you are plenty diversified because your account doesn't have MORE risk than the market as a whole. And, as we've repeated 394 times, if we look at a long enough timeline, that risk has historically not existed.

It's analogous to coaching a basketball game. You wouldn't draft fast, medium, and slow players to make sure your team was "diversified" across player running speeds. Instead, you'd look to find as many fast players as you could, but you'd try to get fast players who play different positions—point guard, center, shooting guard, etc.—to give you a balanced team that could match whatever your opponents do. It's the same idea here: Owning equities is committing to having fast players, while owning different sectors, styles, and locations ensures you have players at different and complementary positions.

Let's use an example. Asset allocation is achieved when you own fifty shares of Amazon stock and $10K worth of Amazon bonds. Yes, you are allocated between asset classes (stocks and bonds), but you are not *diversified*, as you are tied exclusively to Amazon. (And it's not that relevant which company it is. I'm using Amazon for both to illustrate the point, but the real issue is that all your stock market exposure is through one company.)

You achieve diversification by owning $2K of Amazon, $2K of Berkshire Hathaway, $2K of Google, $2K of Johnson & Johnson, $2K of Procter & Gamble, $2K of Nike, and $2K of hundreds of other companies. Yes, you are entirely invested in equities, but you are diversified because you are not tied to the fortunes of one company, strategy, or idea. If Nike gets crushed next quarter but the broader market is up, the rest of your portfolio won't be affected much. If you *only* owned Nike, however, it wouldn't matter much what the rest of the stock market did!

In this example, you are successfully utilizing the asset class that has historically provided the greatest long-term return (equities), but you are doing so in a way that doesn't concentrate you in any one company or approach. This means if one company isn't doing so well, the others will make up for it.

(And in case this isn't clear, these are just examples, not stock recommendations! I'm just using big names as they tend to be helpful for illustrative purposes.)

If we're saying it's foolish to "diversify just for the sake of owning more stuff," you might have a follow-up question: The US stock market has outperformed the international stock market consistently over the last decade, so why would we bother to own international stocks? (And we do!)

Answer: Because these things go in cycles. As we all probably know, between 2010 and 2025, the US stock market has significantly outperformed international stocks. But the previous decade tells a different story: From 2000 to 2010, international stocks outperformed US stocks.[23]

International vs. US Stocks: Rolling Five-Year Difference in Returns

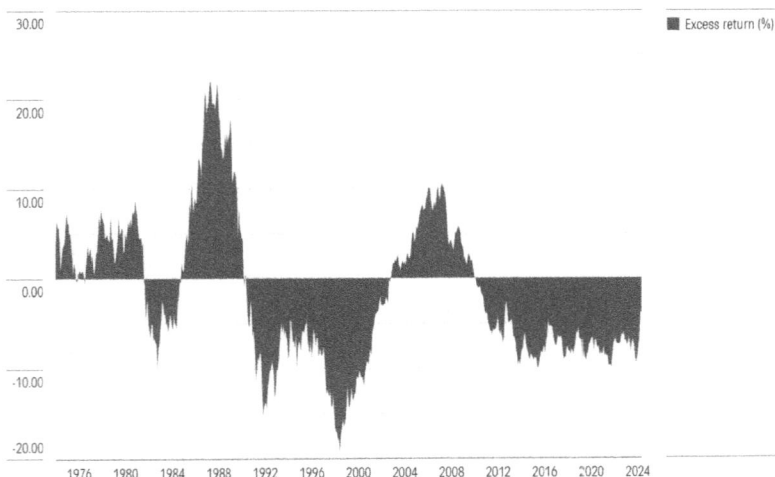

Source: Morningstar Direct. Data as of May 31, 2025. International returns are based on the MSCI EAFE Index

Historically, as well, during periods when the entire stock market lost money, international stocks consistently outperformed their US peers. This means that during those frustrating times when we all bemoan the stock market's losses, international stocks have historically gone down less and are thus exactly what we want during that time.

To be clear, throughout history, US stocks have often outperformed international stocks (though not as dramatically as the last ten years have made it seem). That's why the core of Drucker Wealth's investment approach is made up of US equities. All I'm saying here is that everything has its place, and the ebbs and flows of various equity asset classes are kind of the point!

The beauty of proper diversification isn't just about reducing risk—it's about optimizing your portfolio for long-term success, no matter what the market throws your way. Think of it like a well-balanced sports team: You don't need superstars in every position, but you do need solid performers who complement each other's strengths. Some years, your international stocks might be the MVP while your domestic holdings warm the bench. In other seasons, your small-cap equities might carry the team while your blue chips take a breather. What matters isn't which particular asset class wins the championship each year, but that your collective portfolio keeps scoring points season after season. (Okay, I might have stretched the sports metaphor a bit too far there.)

And speaking of keeping score, let's talk about how we should be measuring and thinking about investment success in the first place.

18

Investing: Total Return Is What Matters

"Calling someone who trades actively in the market an investor is like calling someone who repeatedly engages in one-night stands a romantic."
– Warren Buffett

People often think their home is their "best" investment. It's probably not. The reason people default to assuming that is because it's the only investment that they bought, held, and left alone for thirty years! Not checking or thinking about your home value for literal decades is a big part of the story.

Think about it: If you bought a home thirty years ago for $400K and today it's worth $1.2M . . . that *sounds* amazing, right? Just look at all those gains on what started out as a relatively small investment. The numbers are eye-popping at first glance.

But the truth is, you've averaged about a 3.7% annual rate of return. It just *feels* like more than that because you allowed time to compound your money in a way that you don't with any of your other investments. In other words, you didn't obsessively check your gains every month, so you get the benefit of focusing only on these large, round numbers—the small amount at the beginning and the large amount at the end. That same money ($400K) invested in the S&P 500 at that time would be worth $9.4M! That's almost 10x more! (We are not saying that this hypothetical person shouldn't have lived in their hypothetical home . . . it's just to illustrate the point.)

But what would earning that growth have required from you? Well, it would have required . . .

- That you didn't get nervous and sell out your portfolio when it lost 20% of its value (which would have happened at least four to five times over the course of the thirty years).

- That you didn't get impatient and take money out of the portfolio to fund a trip, renovate your home, or buy a new car.

- That you didn't repeatedly move funds around to find the specific sector that was outperforming the rest of the market.

In short, you would have to treat your investment portfolio the same way you treat the equity in your home.

Don't think about it. Don't look at it. Don't consider it available to withdraw for any reason. Don't worry about the year-to-year fluctuations. Just let it sit over there in the corner, out of mind from your daily life! (By the way, as we'll discuss in the next chapter, this is NOT an argument against buying that house. You need to live somewhere, and that home may be the greatest return on lifestyle you've ever had. We're simply using the example to illustrate a larger point about behavioral investing.)

Think about it this way: We all seem to intuitively understand that the market value of our home really doesn't matter unless we are planning to sell. Who even knows what your home can sell for until you're getting ready to move? Yet we always seem to know the market value and performance of our investment portfolios . . . when we should be treating them the exact same way. If you are not trying to sell—because this money is set aside for long-term future goals and you understand your investment purpose—we should not be concerned with the day-to-day performance.

The takeaway? Sometimes, the expectations that we subconsciously assign to our assets play a much larger role in how we think they're doing than the performance numbers themselves. And this makes sense, because financial planning does not take place on a spreadsheet.

So, the next time you find yourself comparing investment returns with your brother-in-law at Thanksgiving dinner (we all have that relative who somehow doubled their money on some obscure cryptocurrency), remember this: Moment-in-time numbers rarely tell the whole story. Your financial journey isn't about having the most impressive performance chart at any given moment. It's about building a comprehensive strategy that delivers what matters: sustainable growth that funds the life you want to live.

Speaking of major decisions that impact your total financial picture . . . let's look at what is likely the biggest purchase you'll ever make: a home.

19

Home Ownership: Our (Primary) Home– Buying Philosophy

"Too many people spend money they earned to buy things they don't want to impress people they don't like."
– Will Rogers

My philosophy around (primary) home buying can be boiled down to this: Your primary residence is first and foremost a place to live, not a vehicle for growing your wealth. That doesn't mean buying a home is a bad financial move—far from it. But the decision to buy, where to buy, and how much to spend should be driven by lifestyle considerations first, with a focus on how much you will one day make from its sale, a distant (if not totally ignored) component of the decision.

The financial choices you make as a homebuyer have the power to either accelerate your path to financial independence or derail it—which means that this might be the most important chapter in this book.

Think about it: For most of you, your mortgage payment is your largest monthly expense, the purchase price (by far) the most you've ever spent on anything, and your housing decisions will influence nearly every other financial choice you make—from how much you can save, to where your kids go to school, to how much you spend on transportation and maintenance.

Get this decision right, and you create a foundation for everything else we've discussed. Get it wrong, and you're fighting an uphill battle on a driveway that's way too steep.

With the following seven principles, I'll walk you through exactly how to think about home buying in a way that balances your lifestyle desires with your long-term financial goals.

1. Spend Less on Your House: You May (Will!) Be Happier

Admittedly, this first note is anecdotal and not scientific. The rest of this piece will provide numbers, ratios, and facts. But before we discuss this intellectually, I'd be doing you a disservice if I didn't break down some of the effects of different home-buying decisions, based on my experience and my gut. Because that's what buying a home is—an emotional, all-encompassing gut decision—and to help guide that decision, I can tell you what I know to be true from our team's collective experience of more than ONE HUNDRED YEARS of working with clients.

Keeping up with the Joneses is a real thing. Feeling like we need to buy a certain level of home because that's what our friends/colleagues/neighbors have done has unfortunately become ingrained in our DNA. I can't tell you how many times I've heard clients say, "I can't find anything below $1.5M or $2M or (insert number here), so that's my starting number." Well, maybe you can't buy a home that checks all ten of your boxes for anything less than $2M (for example), but you can find one that satisfies your four deal-breakers for $1.5M. Financial decision-making is always about prioritizing what's most important to you in a number of different areas (e.g., housing, travel, family, retirement, and charity) and being uncompromising in what's most important so you can achieve your version of success across the board.

Team Drucker takes pride in being "brutally honest." Housing is probably the conversation where this mostly comes into play. So, here's my brutal honesty: Buying a home out of their price range is the single biggest reason I see people thrown off the track toward their long-term goals. That one decision has more power than any other to create financial uncertainty and anxiety.

And on the flip side, doing it right can lead to an incredible degree of financial flexibility.

My dad is my role model in his approach to life, family, and business. His personal finances are no different. He is financially independent and has been for some time. He bought his current home—the house where my sister and I grew up in—twenty-five years ago. It's a fine house . . . but it was an amazing home. It was both a wonderful place to grow up *AND* the monthly costs fit comfortably in my parents' budget twenty-five years ago—which means that the economics have only gotten better as their income and net worth grew over time.

They could have bought a bigger or nicer home over the years (just ask my mom), or they could have dumped hundreds of thousands of dollars in renovations, but my dad never saw the point. The house was a place to live and raise a family. Nothing more. He didn't derive validation from how big his house was, or how "new" the kitchen was, or whether it was the nicest home on the block. He just didn't care. (My house was also *the* house where all our friends in the neighborhood hung out, in part because it wasn't a museum . . . it was lived in. I do think these points are related.)

I can confidently say that my parents' house was substantially "less" than what they could afford and has been for over two decades. In the years since they bought it, it would have been easy, quite frankly, for them to spend a lot more . . . with nary an effect on their finances. But when I would bring this up to my dad every now and then and ask if he ever thought about buying bigger, he would answer, "To what end?" The fact that the house never felt like a financial albatross around my parents' necks gave them peace of mind when they were starting out and raising a young family. They never had that feeling of swimming upstream or needing their income to chase their lifestyle. They always felt in control.

A 2025 update: Since I wrote this, my parents *did* buy a much larger home, which they love. It's awesome! It's where we celebrate family holidays (they have three grandkids, with hopefully a bunch more to come), and my dad built out a Brazilian Jiu-Jitsu studio in the carriage house where all his friends come over a few times each week to train. And this decision supports everything we've been discussing in this book. They were able to do this now because of the decisions they made earlier that set them up for their current stage of life. A "bigger" home back then wouldn't have provided as much joy and meaning as it does for the entire family now.

A home is the single biggest thing you will ever buy and own. My parents aced this big decision, which allowed them to spend money on the family in other ways, such as family trips, summer camps, tennis and basketball lessons, a full gym in the basement—things they found immensely more valuable. And they were able to execute them without guilt, debate, or doubt.

So what should you take away from my dad's story? First, don't buy a home based on the assumption that your income will go up forever and ever, and you'll one day have more breathing room than you do now. It might be true (as it was for my dad), but there's a difference between *wanting* your income to go up and *needing* it to go up to avoid crashing out financially.

Instead, approach the buying process by assuming your income increases will be more muted. If you only make a tiny amount more each year, would you still feel comfortable buying that home? What if your living expenses go up 5–10% with each additional child you have? What if you commit to traveling more as a family as you get older? What if your travel budget increases from $10K annually to $20K? Would the home costs start to make you sweat? My point: Give yourself some breathing room. Buy a home that doesn't require every other financial decision you make to go perfectly . . . because as we all know, they probably won't.

Your future self will thank you.

2. What You Can Get Approved for Isn't What You Should Spend

An approval for a mortgage amount is not a suggestion— it is an upper limit. It is literally the most you are allowed to borrow to buy a home, but it should have absolutely no bearing on what you actually spend.

It doesn't account for your fixed expenses, variable expenses, future schooling costs, or level of liquidity. It doesn't reflect whether you need to play catch-up in saving toward retirement, whether you have plans of going from a two- to a one-income household, whether you plan on having more kids, changing careers, starting a business, and so on. All these future costs, goals, and decisions should be considered together, holistically, allowing you to understand how your housing purchase will impact the bigger picture.

As a rule of thumb, we maintain that your all-in housing costs (e.g., mortgage, interest, property taxes, HOA, and condo fees) should equate to less than 20% of your household's gross income. (For example: If you make $500K, your total housing costs should come out to less than $100K.) Of course, this is just a way to start the conversation about housing costs, rather than a hard-and-fast rule. Sometimes you can achieve this ratio but still be left in a vulnerable position.

For example, maybe the house you're looking to buy would only cost you 17% of your current gross income each year. That's below the target—*but* if your *current* housing costs only equate to 8%, it might still be more than the rest of your plan can handle. You've effectively turned the strength of your plan (having low housing costs) into more of a push. If you already have a low savings rate, this increase very well might push your spending past its breaking point and damage the long-term viability of your plan. And all this could happen even if the housing costs by themselves don't break the bank!

Some of our clients have fantastic savings rates, saving or investing at least 25% of their gross income annually, chiefly because their housing costs are so low relative to their income. Thinking this savings rate means they're untouchable, they might ask us to run the plan with MUCH larger housing costs. But our estimates show that doubling or tripling their housing costs by buying the bigger home might push that 25% savings rate the plan is counting on into the single digits. And again, because housing will most likely be both your single largest and your longest-running annual expense, its effect on the plan—whether positive or negative—is usually exponential.

3. Total Purchase Price Is What Matters

I've had dozens of conversations with clients discussing a home they really like, but which might be a bit out of their price range based on the rest of their financial program. Naturally, part of my role is to let them know how and why the purchase might be problematic, to what degree, etc. Quite a few of these clients have followed up on this conversation by asking if they could increase their down payment (over and above the 20% we discussed) as a way to lower their monthly costs.

Now, figuring out the right balance between down payment and mortgage is an important conversation to have, assuming you can afford the purchase price. But moving the costs around in this way (so that you're paying more upfront instead of higher monthly costs) most likely won't do much to change the calculus of whether you can afford the home in the first place. Lowering your monthly costs may help you to feel better about your purchase because you don't have to see these higher monthly costs bump up against your paychecks every single month, but if you're just taking more out of your liquid net worth (in the form of a larger down payment) to get to that result, it can have the same effect!

If you're buying a $1.5M house and instead of putting down $300K (20%), you want to put down $500K (30%) to lower your monthly expense, you need to pull out an ADDITIONAL $200K from your savings/investments. While it might feel better to rip the band-aid off at the start like this, think about what that money could be doing for you if it stayed available to you long-term. That money could have been invested, set aside in tax-efficient retirement accounts, allocated to the kids' college accounts, or earmarked for other goals down the road. Quite simply, there's a huge opportunity cost for putting down that "extra" money upfront.

Erasing years of cash accumulation and investment savings in one fell swoop like this can ultimately have the same net effect as if you put down less and instead had higher monthly costs that eat up your saving potential over time. And while seeking to lower your monthly costs might "feel" better (and I absolutely understand that impulse), in either case, you're limiting the growth of your other capital by extending yourself on the house's purchase price . . . however you choose to pay for it.

To be clear, deciding whether to put more or less down depending on interest rates, investment opportunity costs, etc., is a worthwhile separate conversation about asset placement—and sometimes it *does* make sense to put more than usual down. My point here is that you should be aware that opting to do this might be an emotional rationalization to make yourself feel comfortable buying a home that's outside your price range. At the end of the day, the total purchase price is what matters when determining whether you can afford a home, not the way you may choose to pay for it. When running your numbers, I prefer to calculate your income-to-housing ratio as compared to your current housing costs using a 20% down payment figure, as this forces us to compare apples to apples and prevents us from manipulating the monthly numbers to SEEM better than they are.

4. Your Home Is a Place to Live

Every now and then, a client will rationalize a home purchase price (or the renovation costs that will follow) by saying, "Well, it's an investment!" Perhaps, but historically . . . not a very good one! Real estate prices have gone up approximately 4% over time.[24] And that's to say nothing of the property taxes, maintenance costs, insurance costs, etc., that you pay along the way, which don't factor into the sales price but do affect the total net return. And to take it one step further: In our experience, when you ultimately do sell your home, you'll probably be using the proceeds from the sale to buy your next home. Any gains you receive at the point of sale aren't necessarily going to be reinvested— they're going to help you pay for your next place to live. And that's really the way I'd recommend thinking of your primary residence: It's a place to live. And you are always going to need a place to live.

Of course, there are exceptions. You buy in a hot neighborhood, and the purchase price increases dramatically over three years, giving you an opportunity to sell. This happens! But buying a home with the assumption of wild appreciation would mean banking on the outlier rather than the historical norm.

As I've already said, my point is not that you shouldn't have bought and lived in that house over the last twenty years. That's ridiculous! You need to live somewhere, and quality of life is SUPER important. The house will likely have served you wonderfully over that time. The point is exactly that: It's a place to live and shouldn't be thought of (or relied upon) as an investment that will support your future income needs.

5. There's No Rush to Buy . . . Do So on Your Own Timeline!

This point is geared toward our clients who are thinking about buying their FIRST primary residence. When I ask clients why they want to buy a home, and their timeline for doing so, I often hear, "I just want to start building equity . . . I feel ridiculous paying all this rent!" And I can understand this thought process! In fact, it seems to be a core part of the American ethos. Buying a home ASAP has always been interpreted as a clear sign that you're "on track" and "starting your life." But that's not *always* the case.

Let's start by understanding how much "equity" you're actually building when you buy a home. On average, only 30% of your annual housing costs go toward your mortgage principal (i.e., building equity).[25] The rest goes toward mortgage interest, property taxes, insurance, maintenance, and such. So most of the money you spend each month has the same practical effect as money you would have paid toward rent. You are not getting it back.

By way of example: Using current mortgage rates, a **$2M home with 20% down** will cost you **$3,832,920 over thirty years** (based on the mortgage and interest alone)! Over the first four years of owning this home, you will have paid **$431,073 in interest** but built up only about **$79K in equity** (before any appreciation). Of course, interest rates will fluctuate, so these numbers will be different depending on your year of purchase (and who knows where interest rates will be when you read this book to your grandchildren forty years from now!). The point is just to emphasize that sometimes the idea of building equity seems a lot better than the actual amount of equity you might be building year-to-year.

Now, of course, if you could pay $10K per month in all-in housing costs for a place you own or a place you rent, all else being equal, you'd rather own it (and yes, there is the mortgage interest deduction to benefit from as well!). Building some equity slowly is better than none at all.

But let's remember: Spending $10K on a home you rent versus one you buy usually means two totally different "levels" of house! A home you rent for $10K is going to be a lot nicer/bigger than one you can buy for $10K, since it usually costs more to buy a home (all extra costs included) than it would to rent that same home or apartment. You might be comfortable (and enjoy yourself!) renting a home that would be out of your price range to buy.

Sometimes renting makes more sense for practical reasons as well. Renting affords you flexibility. It gives you the freedom to pick up in twelve months and say, "I'm out of here, I want to go live in a different part of town," or "I might be leaving my job in two years, and I want to find a

159

remote opportunity so I can move closer to family." As a renter, you can change course on a dime.

Personally, that's why I have rented while living in New York City. Throughout my twenties and early thirties, I didn't know where I'd find myself five to seven years out. Even today, I know my family sometimes talks about moving to other parts of the country. I know that my wife and I don't want to live in NYC long-term, even though it's where we happen to be right now (this will probably be dated within six months!). I know that not once while I've been living in New York City have I even thought about buying a home, even though, based on my personal finances, I could have. The future optionality that renting has provided me during this stage of my life has been of substantially higher value, measured in peace of mind and opportunity cost, than I would have gained from the equity of a home—and that's to say nothing of the fact that renting is just easier than being a homeowner.

I mention a five-to-seven-year plan because that is typically the break-even point at which it makes sense to buy. If you don't see yourself living in the home for at least five to seven years, the costs of buying (like closing costs, broker fees, moving costs, and furniture) mean that renting might make more sense over that shorter time period.

Not to belabor the point, but renting also doesn't require a down payment. So, while I'm figuring out my long-term plan over these handful of years and not locking up any down payment capital, I'm able to save 30% of my income every single month into my long-term investments and retirement accounts. This allows me to build my net worth through saving and investing so that when I am ready to buy, the down payment I ultimately make won't capsize my liquidity.

6. Do Not Forget About Property Taxes . . . They Don't Go Away!

As I mentioned, my sister, Gabby, and I grew up in a great area in North New Jersey with excellent schools. My town was wonderful; I'd recommend it to anyone. But here's an interesting thing about it: There's one part of town called The Hill that, for some ungodly reason, has property taxes double what my parents paid. Just recently, my dad ran into someone who lives in that part of town. They got to talking about the area, and the guy asked my dad what his property taxes were. My dad cautioned this guy that he didn't want to know . . . it would get him too worked up!

As I don't think he's a reader, I'll lay it out: My dad pays $17K each year in property taxes, whereas this guy (let's call him Greg) pays upward of $45K! That's $45K per year he will never get back. For some reason, people get more worked up about having to pay income taxes than property taxes (even though the former is a lot more logical . . . but that's a separate conversation!). Imagine if your tax bill each year resulted in an extra $28K liability each April— you'd be livid! As my dad is fond of saying, our family and

Greg's family went to the same school system, the garbage got picked up the same day, the police and fire department worked the same way, and we all knew the same people.

Property taxes don't go away when you pay off your mortgage, either. They're with you for life. Underestimate their effect at your own peril.

7. Expect Maintenance Costs

When mapping out a potential home purchase for a client, we always want to make sure we accurately account for maintenance costs. Obviously, we have no idea what exactly this will come to, but 1% to 2% of the total home value annually is a good rule of thumb. So, if your home is worth $1M, then we would want to figure in $10K to $20K in maintenance costs each year. Of course, just like with investment returns, the average doesn't tell you anything about any given year, only that the costs over time should revert to that average. Some years, you might need to fix up the kitchen, replace the washing machine, or repair a leak. Other years, the maintenance costs may be more minimal or run-of-the-mill. All the same, 1–2% is a good planning assumption.

I'll also caution that this is how buying a "bigger, more expensive" home has a negative compounding effect. Typically, the more expensive your home, the more expensive it is to fix, clean, and maintain. Lawn care is more expensive. Utilities are more expensive. Heat and air conditioning. Plumbing. Cleaning services. Upkeep. Literally everything is a bigger task, and therefore, it costs more money to maintain. That home you thought you were just barely extending yourself for becomes a lot more expensive in five years, when all the other costs start to compound. And these costs typically only go up with time. Simply put, annual housing costs are NEVER just what you're paying in mortgage and property taxes.

Last anecdote on the subject: A friend assumed that buying a house built in 2015 was going to save her all those staggering maintenance costs her friends were experiencing with their older houses—a completely new A/C system, replacing wood floors, a roof repair. But guess what? It didn't. All the little maintenance issues and renos she had to do in the first year ended up being just as expensive . . . just for different reasons!

I want to close with an important clarification: None of this is to argue that you shouldn't dream of having your own home—and dream big. We have helped dozens of clients plan for and then buy their dream home; there are very few parts of what I do that are more rewarding! I'm just saying that you shouldn't feel pressured just because it "seems" like the right thing to do. Like everything else, when it comes to financial decision-making, we want to make intentional housing decisions that balance your current and future priorities.

20

Home Ownership: Paying Off Your Mortgage

"The only thing more stressful than buying a home is owning a home."
– Anonymous

I get various versions of this question all the time:

- "Should I use my annual bonus to pay down the mortgage balance?"
- "Should I be putting more toward my mortgage each month?"
- "Should I use my excess emergency reserves to pay off my remaining mortgage balance?"

The answer depends entirely on your personal circumstances, but for the majority of our mid-career professionals, I would argue the answer is an emphatic, *"Probably not (but, also, it depends)!"*

First, let's discuss when paying off your mortgage or aggressively paying your monthly bills is the no-doubt-about-it wrong move. If paying off your mortgage leaves you with too small of an emergency reserve or not enough in the bank to pay for those large expenses you have coming over the next few years (like planning for a baby, helping family, or taking time off from work), then it's absolutely not worth making the extra mortgage payment. You will be leaving yourself with too small a margin for error.

You have a mortgage in the first place so you can take care of your other financial responsibilities while simultaneously paying for your home. *Stay the course.* Similarly, if paying down your mortgage would prevent you from contributing enough to your 401(k)/403b to receive the employer match or to maximize your tax deduction, then again, I'd say it's not worth it. I would argue that you're effectively just robbing Peter to pay Paul—you're just moving money around.

When it comes to missing your window to contribute to retirement accounts, you don't get to make up for lost time. Think of your annual contributions to retirement accounts like filling up a bucket: You can only ever fill it to the top each year, regardless of what you did the year before. Given this, we want to be intentional about how much and when we add to these accounts. For example, in 2026 you could contribute up to $24,500 into your 401(k)—so if you only contributed $6K, you'd be leaving $18,500 on the table that could have been contributed. Maybe it doesn't make sense to contribute the full amount based on your cash flow, but we at least want to make sure we're considering extra mortgage payments in the context of this broader plan.

Now, let's assume you're in excellent financial shape and can pay off your mortgage without impacting how much you're adding to other investments and retirement accounts. If that's the case, does it make sense? Well, *typically, still NO! (But again, it depends . . . Isn't personal finance fun?)*

Let's assume you bought your home sometime between 2005 and 2018. You probably have a "low" mortgage rate (I would call anything under 5% low). The question then is: Could that $100K that you've built up and are thinking of using to pay off your mortgage be allocated in a way that will grow at a rate higher than your mortgage (in this example, let's say 4%)? That's really what we're talking about: opportunity cost. In other words, what else could you be doing with that $100K lump sum if you didn't put it toward your mortgage? If you have a low interest rate, we should be thinking about your mortgage not as a liability that needs to be paid off as soon as possible, but as an asset to keep in your back pocket for as long as you can so your money can work more effectively elsewhere.

I'll put it like this: If I can pay the bank 3.5% on my mortgage each month, but my capital investments are earning 7% average returns, why would I be in a rush to change that arrangement? That's free money!

Only paying the minimum required on my mortgage each month allows me to continue investing my cash into higher-performing assets. Again, it's a fantastic feeling to know that you *could* pay off your mortgage at any time (and that should be the working goal), but whether to go ahead and pay it off is a decision that's more about opportunity cost and financial return.

And one final point on the side of not paying it off sooner than necessary: If you *pay only the amount that's required,* you maintain your flexibility. Choosing not to pay off your mortgage today doesn't eliminate any of your options. *You can still choose to pay it off tomorrow!*

If, however, you choose to pay it off today and you end up needing additional cash sooner than you thought, you'll be strapped for cash and might need to take out a line of credit, a home equity line, or other unsavory and unpredictable debt options. From a liquidity standpoint, I'd always rather have that cash or investment in my back pocket, with the opportunity to pay off my mortgage within shouting distance, than the other way around.

So, when *should* we explore paying off your mortgage? First off, if you have a high interest rate and can't refinance, then the opportunity cost of not being able to reinvest your money isn't so high. In that case, it might be worth the peace of mind to eliminate the debt. In fact, the concept of financial peace of mind brings us to the real reason it might sometimes make sense to pay off your mortgage: If it would make you happier to be debt-free.

Financial planning is way more art than science.

Some people can't stand debt of any kind and are super motivated to pay it off. It's one less thing for them to worry about. While I would (and just did) make the logical and financial argument that mortgages can be the "good" kind of debt that is more "asset" than "liability," your financial feelings don't have to be rational! Suppose even after walking through your current cash flow, debt, and opportunity-cost position, you're still committed to paying off the mortgage— we'd help you do so! Maybe that means paying off a little bit more each month or using your bonus to take off an extra 5% each year—or maybe it really does mean paying off the mortgage entirely so you can enjoy being debt-free.

21

Real Estate Investing: The Allure vs. the Reality

"A good rule of thumb is that nothing in need of constant repair and requiring a half-dozen commissioned middlemen will yield superior investing results."

– Morgan Housel

Each week, I get a dozen calls from professionals reaching out to see if we might be a good fit to help them with their planning and investing. On these calls, I get to hear about their financial dreams, their family and financial dynamics, areas where they think they could use some help, and what they've been doing thus far, both financially and professionally. I love learning about so many different perspectives and hearing so many people's money stories. Unfortunately, these calls also give me a glimpse into how financial media, TikTok, and Instagram creep into people's thinking about their money. Every so often, I hear smart, sophisticated professionals ask about getting involved in rental properties to generate passive income, even though they have absolutely no interest or experience in real estate itself. I can't help but share that my reaction to this is akin to when you're watching a horror movie and you see the monster creep up behind the main character. It's that feeling of wanting to yell at the TV to make sure the character gets out of the way.

First, I wonder how much they've thought through the logistics and details, or if it just *sounds* like something they *should* want. And when I ask a few follow-up questions, it typically turns out to be just that—something they felt almost obligated to ask about, more as a general inquiry rather than something they're genuinely interested in.

I think one reason young people are drawn to the idea of securing passive income via rental properties is because it's been presented as this easy life-hack strategy that leads to all the passive income you could ever want, so that by forty-five, you're able to leave the rat race forever. (The second most common motivation I hear revolves around the tax benefits that come with real estate investing.) You hear the Instagram version of rental real estate, and you start to think, "Well, if I could have enough income coming in each month to cover my expenses, such as rent and groceries, then I would be able to stop working. I could live off my rental income and do what I really want."

You can probably tell from my framing that I think this is mostly a dangerous, impractical mirage! I'll explain why—but before I get too comfortable on my soapbox, let me just say what should be obvious: Yes, it is possible to be profitable in real estate rentals and have this all work out beautifully. Of course. I am not saying it can't work. I just think it's something that most people should not get involved in, and it carries significantly more risk than upside for almost everyone who mentions it to me.

My own experience with clients has shown me that people who are successful in the rental real estate game have three things in common:

1. They treat it as both a business and a job—meaning they dedicate meaningful time to the activity and

went into it already having the applicable skills and knowledge of real estate.

2. They had a sizable net worth (at least $3M+) in cash and investments *before* they decided to get involved in any capital-intensive real estate projects.

3. They (or their family) own a number of properties and have operated them for a long time. This is essentially a combination of #1 and #2, but what we're really saying here is that they own real estate at scale. They are not trying to generate passive income by owning a single property or two; they are running a business in which their dozen properties are productive for them in the aggregate. It's a numbers game (especially if they consider leverage to be a big part of the strategy).

On the flip side, I have genuinely never seen it work out for the type of family we most commonly work with. When you have one spouse in big tech, one spouse working as a physician (or in finance, as an attorney, etc.), and they're earning a combined $600K, with three kids and limited time outside of family and work responsibilities . . . buying one or two random rental properties for extra income just does not make sense.

Let's consider what this might look like in practice. Imagine you want to buy a $600K property and turn it into an income-generating rental. You decide to put 20% down and finance the remaining $480K. That means we'll be taking $120K out of your liquid/investable net worth and moving it into a more illiquid/unavailable vehicle. (We'll come back to this.) Let's assume this is your entire upfront cost. (Though of course, it probably wouldn't be. There would be closing costs, advertising costs, maintenance and fix-up work costs, furniture refurbishments, and so on before you could rent it out—but let's keep it simple for the sake of this example.) Now you need to find renters. Let's say you get lucky again and find some immediately, so there isn't an extended period where you're paying the mortgage without receiving rent back . . . that's great!

A thirty-year $600K mortgage at a 5.5% rate would run you approximately $2,725 per month. You will need to charge more than that to squeeze out that additional cash flow. But wait. You also need to account for property taxes and insurance, factor in future vacancies, and build in enough margin to cover the maintenance work and costs that will inevitably come up over time. At a conservative estimate, you might need to charge about 30% more than the rent in order to break even and successfully "run" the rental. So now you no longer need to charge $2,725—you need to charge $3,543 before you can start feeling like you truly have "extra" income your family can benefit from. (And remember, that's just the amount needed to break even. We're not even at positive cash flow yet!)

You might be thinking that even if the rental doesn't bring in a huge amount of income, you're still covering your mortgage, which means the renters are effectively paying your mortgage. *"It's costing me nothing to build up my home equity!"*

Here's the thing, though: It's not costing you nothing! It's costing you the opportunity cost of not doing something else with that initial $120K down payment, and the growth on the $2,725 (plus property taxes, maintenance, money set aside for vacant months, etc.) every single month! What else could that money be doing? Put even more directly: Is the capital outlay ultimately going to grow at a better rate than if you had invested that same amount elsewhere?

Let's look into that! (I know we've discussed the stock market's performance throughout the book, but I want to run through it here so we can really understand it in relation to real estate. Bear with me!)

As shown in the chart, the S&P 500 has averaged approximately 10% annualized rate of return over the last fifty years. Home prices have risen by only about 4% per year.* Assuming these historical rates of return, $100K put into the capital markets will equal about $2.34M in thirty years, whereas that same $100K put into a house will be worth approximately $324K when you're ready to sell in thirty years. Feel free to assume the stock market will do worse than its historical return, and that real estate will do a bit better. It doesn't change the overall takeaway!

*Yes, I understand the "leverage" argument: You put $120K down and the property appreciates from $600K to $630K, leaving you with a $30K gain on your initial $120K deposit. I get it. I think

Best Asset Classes

BY DECADE!

Data from NYU. Annualized returns. (Stocks = S&P 500, Cash = 3-month T-bills, Bonds = 10 year Treasuries, Real Estate = Case-Shiller Index, Gold = Year-End Price per oz, Inflation = CPI)

	Stocks	Cash	Bonds	Real Estate	Gold	Inflation
1930s	-0.9%	1.0%	4.0%	-1.2%	5.3%	-2.0%
1940s	8.5%	0.5%	2.5%	8.1%	-0.8%	5.4%
1950s	19.5%	2.0%	0.8%	3.0%	1.0%	2.2%
1960s	7.7%	4.0%	2.4%	2.2%	1.6%	2.5%
1970s	5.9%	6.3%	5.4%	8.7%	28.6%	7.4%
1980s	17.3%	8.8%	12.0%	5.9%	-2.5%	5.1%
1990s	18.0%	4.8%	7.4%	2.7%	-3.1%	2.9%
2000s	-1.0%	2.7%	6.3%	4.0%	14.1%	2.6%
2010s	13.4%	0.6%	4.1%	3.8%	3.4%	1.8%
2020s	11.9%	1.9%	-2.4%	10.2%	8.0%	4.5%
Average	10.3%	3.3%	4.3%	4.7%	5.6%	3.2%

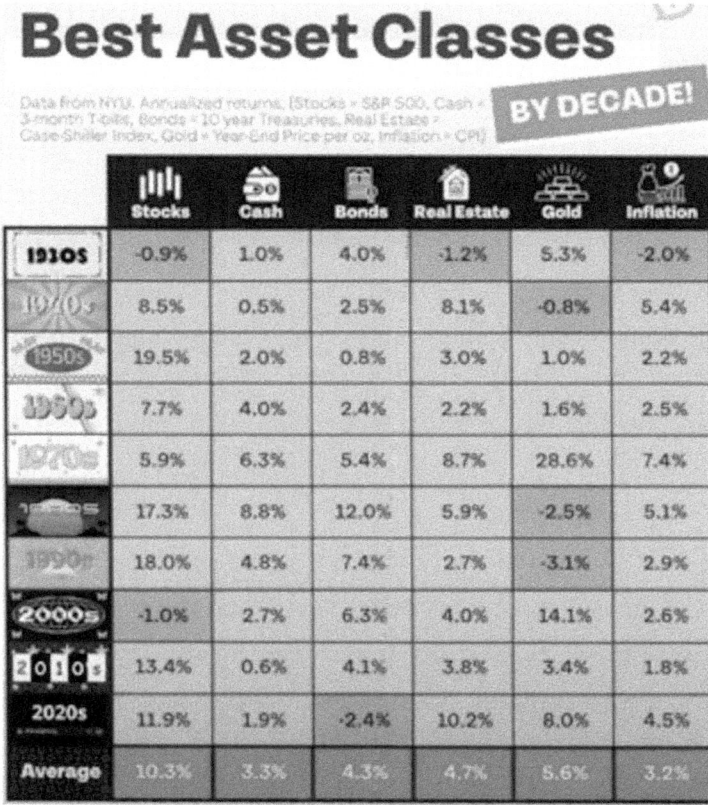

leverage can work in the aggregate when you have a dozen properties and you're consistently buying/selling multiple properties over
short periods of time, using the leveraged gains for re-investment and
leveling up. And as is my overarching point, this isn't what we're
discussing here. That is a real estate business.

If we're talking about buying ONE rental property and
you're keeping the property for years to come (as you would
be if the motivation is to generate passive income), this is a lot
less impactful because each mortgage payment means a greater

share of any potential appreciation is the return of your own money (and not leverage).

Add to that the interest payments, property tax payments, and the maintenance you pay each year (and that isn't reflected in the superficial equation comparing the down payment to the appreciation of the property's value), and ultimately, I land in the same place.

Don't get me wrong. It's possible you will find a property that generates explosive short-term appreciation, greater than what you can find investing in the stock market—but how likely is that? How much risk are you taking on in trying to become the exception to the rule?

And that's not even considering all the costs along the way. You will have paid property taxes, maintenance fees, housing insurance, liability insurance, normal upkeep costs, home improvements, and more. All of this will dramatically lower that 4% even further and hasn't been subtracted from the sale price (though you no longer have that money!).

By "investing" in real estate, you're giving up some dramatic capital appreciation in the hopes that the income you generate will make up for the shortfall. (I'm guessing at the motivation here because—as you might be able to tell—this is not something I'd ever consider doing personally.)

And here's the rub:

Nothing about it is "passive"! It requires more diligence, know-how, and periodic involvement than can reasonably be considered a "passive" activity. Are you committed to doing all the work yourself? Are you running the property, advertising to find tenants, showing the property, vetting applicants, responding to maintenance requests, coordinating the repairs, cleaning and staging before each new guest, answering prospective renter emails, collecting and following up on payments, dealing with any legal issues, and so on?

A real estate broker client once told me that when she talks to her clients about potentially buying a rental property, she always reminds them that doing so would make them a *landlord*! Her point: It is a responsibility! If a pipe bursts, the roof springs a leak, people move out unexpectedly and you have to scramble to find new renters, or your renters don't pay, it's all on you to deal with it.

Of course, the other option is to do none of this yourself and hire a management company. That helps make sure you don't have much work to do, but there is a trade-off: A third party is now cutting into your margins. The standard property management fees run 10% of your monthly rent (to say nothing of losing the tax benefits associated with being a real estate professional). After all that, and even assuming EVERYTHING goes right—how much extra "income" are you really generating each month that's above your costs? $200? $300? $500? We locked up $120K of real capital—money that's now unavailable for your family's other short-term financial goals—and now you have to deal with a management company for an extra $500 per month? For a busy family earning north of $500K per year, I truly don't think that juice, when all is considered, is worth the squeeze!

This chapter isn't meant as a dig at real estate; if anything, it's more a knock on the idea of passive income as a quick-fix replacement for growing your income, compounding your wealth, and building a legacy. Case in point: Have you read those clickbait articles with the headline, "Thirty-Five-Year-Old Jake Has $1.5M and Is Living off His Passive Income!"? I find them endlessly amusing. For starters, what sort of life is Jake living to be able to live off that amount of money for the rest of his life? Because $1.5M is not enough money to be retired for forty years, at least not with any sort of quality of life. (And, as we covered in Part 1, when most people talk about "retirement," they don't mean the literal fact of not having to work; they mean not being at the mercy of a paycheck and getting to live the life they imagine. Being retired is the means, not the end.) Is Jake stretching his $1.5M to last through fifty years of rising costs, while living the life he wants? Ridiculous! Now, of course, those pieces are intentionally extreme and outlandish (to generate clicks), but they're still popular because they touch our human impulse to try and short-circuit the time it takes to build meaningful wealth.

Speaking of legacy-defining wealth, Warren Buffett was once asked why more people didn't follow his sage advice or financial behaviors. He's one of the wealthiest people alive and is constantly explaining what he does publicly. Why not just try to replicate what he's done? His response? "Oh, that's easy. No one wants to get rich slowly." And Warren Buffett knew of what he spoke: 92% of his wealth was attained after he reached age sixty-five . . . **92%!** (To have more fun with this fact: In Morgan Housel's incredible book, *The Psychology of Money,* he references that of Warren Buffett's $84.5 billion net worth, over $81.5 billion came after his mid-sixties . . . it's mind blowing to think about![26])

This brings us to a larger issue with the drive for passive income (whether through real estate or some other avenue): Worrying about income before you're ready to live off your accumulated assets is like training for a marathon and worrying about how you're going to run the twenty-sixth mile during your first few weeks of running.

(As a quick illustration: If you're forty-three years old and you have an investment portfolio of $2M, all we should be focused on is growing that pot of money to a point where you can ONE DAY generate enough income to live off. Setting up your $2M investment to maximize your income TODAY [which always comes at the expense of other goals, like growth] might mean generating $80K annually [4%]. Is that enough to fund your lifestyle indefinitely? I think not!)

If you do feel like you need to increase your household income now (which may be true), rather than buying a rental property, what if you utilized your skills and knowledge to increase your income-earning potential? If neither is truly "passive," all else being equal, I would rather generate additional income through my own skills, while working on my own timeline, with business expenses I can write off, and without being subject to the whims of the housing market or renters.

In fact, I would argue that the most effective way to increase your income is through professional development and acquiring new skills. This can lead to getting paid more at your job, leveling up to a better role (or better job), or consulting on the side.

In building out financial plans and reviewing decades of cash flows for hundreds of clients, I can genuinely say that continuously and gradually increasing your salary, bonus, and commissions is the most meaningful and easiest way to generate additional income and enhance your family's lifestyle. I know this sounds obvious—"Duh, make more money"—but I mention it because sometimes we spend so much time and energy trying to find a "second" or "passive" income source, when it would be far easier to focus our energies on increasing our primary income.

The discipline, optimism, and commitment required to build wealth over time are key to reaching the financial destination we all want. The impetus to generate passive income while you're still in the accumulation phase mostly seems to me to be an attempt to circumvent that process.

And if I can fall back on my most sincerely held financial belief: We all tend to take unnecessary risks to turn a quick profit or generate "passive" income when we don't have any sort of mechanism, like a financial plan, to tell us how we're doing. It's when we're guessing—stumbling around in the dark, unable to see our financial outlook—that we assume the worst and are left feeling like we need a miracle solution.

Most likely, if you're reading this book, you aren't the quick-fix, pie-in-the-sky type! You just need a plan to get from where you are now to where you want to go, and the discipline to stay on that path.

The Real "Cost" of Being a Landlord

When you buy a property with the sole purpose of renting it out, you are hoping you will generate enough rent to offset your own costs. But regardless, that mortgage bill is coming *every single month*. You are the only one responsible for paying back that $400K mortgage loan—it's not dependent on whether you have stable renters. It is YOUR liability. You are solely responsible when a roof leaks, when there's a plumbing issue, when a tenant wants to get out of their lease early, when three nicer, more modern rentals pop up next to you that people prefer, requiring you to upgrade your space, and so on. And those are just the run-of-the-mill headaches!

There's also the possibility of a never-ending nightmare in which you have renters who won't pay rent, a structural issue that takes years to fix, a fight with the local city board, a mold issue (more on this below), a zoning issue, or any of the other soul-sucking problems that can come when dealing with real property and real people. All of this is enough for me to stay permanently away. Even if these are all 1% outlier scenarios, they serve to highlight the mismatched risk/reward of being a landlord. I just don't get it.

True story: My girlfriend (now wife) and I found mold in our last apartment in NYC, so our landlord had to redo the entire bathroom. It took two months, and I don't even know how much money, to fix. The landlord was a doctor in his mid-forties, and while he was a nice guy, he was only available at weird hours of the day because he was always in the ER. I genuinely felt bad reaching out to him about things in the apartment, but, hey, that's the business he was in! He ended up selling the apartment after our lease expired because he no longer wanted to deal with it.

(To give you some more context: He had originally lived in the apartment himself, got a job at a hospital outside of NYC, and decided to keep it and rent it out for a few years. In my anecdotal experience, this is the same outcome I hear EVERY time someone tries to rent out an apartment or home after living in it. Within a few years, they decide they don't want the hassle. And if you're wondering, he decided to sell even before the whole mold issue popped up!)

All that to say, there is so much that can go wrong and devastate even the relatively thin margins you need to earn—and all of it is completely out of your control! I simply cannot fathom taking on all the headaches and hassles that real estate can create for you, all for the sort of returns we're discussing.

How to Generate REAL Passive Income (When You Need To!)

So, what's the alternative? I can instead take that $120K down payment and add it to my broadly diversified investment portfolio, which represents ownership in the world's greatest and most profitable companies.

There is no maintenance or labor to speak of. No property taxes or annoying tenants. No "nightmare" scenario in which I lose my entire investment (at least not based on all available history). Instead, as my investment and/or retirement accounts grow over time and I start to transition into my retirement years, everything starts to come into focus. As part of my investment program, I'll start to prioritize generating income as the primary replacement for the salary that will disappear when I retire. First, I can start by withdrawing the dividends my portfolio has been reinvesting for the past twenty years. Next, I can start drawing down the principal (which will be offset by the fact that my portfolio is still growing, thus replacing the withdrawals over time!). Finally, I would look to move some (not all!) of my growth-oriented accounts into more income-oriented strategies to enhance the guaranteed portion of my income and protect myself in times of down markets.

Just like that, my investment program has turned into passive income when I need it to!

So many people default to wanting "passive income" via rental properties because it seems "easy" and "natural." We all go on vacations. Most of us have rented a home, so we all think we know how "easy" it is to collect a monthly check for doing nothing (we've just been on the other side of that exchange!). On the flip side, very few understand the mechanics of income distribution from one's investment and retirement portfolios. It's just not something we learn, so we don't think about it as a viable income solution.

The irony? This *is* the easy way to grow your net worth and create a future income stream that isn't dependent upon the sweat of your brow. This *is* the way to build a large enough net worth that you can live off of income and principal distributions for the rest of your life.

It's called **capital investing**.

The CEOs of the greatest companies in the world allow you to share proportionally in the growth of their companies, without having to justify your returns or share any of your labor, time, or energy. You get to share in the growth of these companies, helping to move the economy forward just by being a common shareholder.

That is true "passive income." But it takes patience, discipline, and the behavioral fortitude to favor long-term wealth over making a quick buck. Look, I get it. The quick-fix ways of building wealth are something we hear about constantly—whether on social media, the news, or from friends. And we are bombarded with claims about the one "genius" or "secret" idea that will catapult us a decade ahead. But I can tell you that, in all my years of experience working directly with clients, I have never had anyone find financial independence from just one great idea.

All of it is just a distraction from the personal and behavioral financial planning decisions that allow you to achieve your desired financial outcomes over time.

With that in mind—and since we know that making rash decisions like buying a rental property is something people typically do when they feel lost, without a financial roadmap—here are nine questions to ask yourself, which can help you reframe, or get a sense of, how you're doing:

1. Do I have a six-month emergency reserve sitting in a high-yield savings account?
2. Am I saving/investing *at least* 25% of my gross income each year?
3. Am I maxing out my 401(k)? (Or Solo 401[k]/SEP IRA if I'm self-employed?)
4. Am I maxing out my kids' education accounts (if applicable)?
5. Do I have enough life and disability insurance (based on actual calculations) to protect myself and my family if something were to go wrong?
6. Am I on target (90%+ likelihood) to hit my financial goals in the next ten years?

7. Am I on target (80%+ likelihood) to hit my retire-ment goals?

8. Am I utilizing a flexible investment account that allows me to engage in tax loss harvesting?

9. Do I have a backdoor Roth IRA strategy and a strategy for converting pre-tax IRAs over time?

If you're considering buying a rental property for passive income (or engaging any other, seemingly "advanced" [cough, unnecessarily complicated] strategy for making income)—ask yourself these nine questions. And please, if anyone ever tells you, "This is what rich people do, and you can do it, too!" while touting one of these strategies—run for the hills!

These nine questions will help ground you and guide you back to what matters within your financial program. If you can confidently answer "yes" to each of these nine questions, then you should truly feel fantastic about where you stand financially. So go out and enjoy the day! If you can't, well, every financial decision you make should be about *solving* for them!

Up until the VERY last second of writing this book, the next chapter originally covered the tax benefits associated with real estate. I spent PAGES discussing what it means to have Real Estate Professional Status, why it matters on your tax return, and the reason most people can't actu-ally deduct their real estate losses against ordinary income. We also explained the benefit of deducting your losses on your Schedule C, how depreciation works, and what 1031 exchanges and opportunity zones are. But in the end, I deleted the entire section.

Why? Well, first, it read like a textbook because it was all facts, figures, and tax rules. You never need to know a single thing about depreciation, cost segregation studies, 1031 exchanges, and the like—and despite what you might hear from a twenty-five-year-old on TikTok, you are not missing out on ANYTHING.

The real reason, however, is that if you're truly interested in rental real estate and are committed to making it happen, I'm not your guy! You're probably not interested in learning about these tax "benefits" from someone who has no interest in ever owning rental properties and who thinks the tax benefits are overstated. You're going to keep on your real estate journey. Great! For everyone else—those who never had an interest and those who had a passing curiosity that has now been satisfied—we just saved you five pages of mind-numbing boredom. That's a win!

To close, let me say this: You don't need to agree with my entire perspective on real estate investing. Heck, you don't have to agree with any of it! I wanted to accomplish two goals with this chapter. One, to make you realize that investing in real estate is just another investment option . . . it is NOT a panacea or some secret finance hack that will solve all your problems! And I happen to think it's not worth what comes with it. Others might disagree. But let's lower the temperature here. Second, as always, I want to help you think about what you're doing and why so you can be intentional in your decision-making.

Over the last few chapters, we've covered how to optimize your investments and home purchase decisions . . . but even the most brilliant investment plan can be derailed by life's unexpected events. That's why it's vital to turn our attention to something many high earners consistently overlook: protecting what you've built.

22

Life Insurance:
How Much Protection
Does Your Family Need?

*"Whatever excuses you may have for
not buying life insurance now will only
sound ridiculous to your widow."*
– Anonymous

Here's a truth that might surprise you: Most high-earning professionals I meet are dangerously underinsured. It's not because they're trying to cut corners or save money—it's because they simply don't realize how much protection their family needs.

That tech executive with the perfectly allocated portfolio? The surgeon couple with the tax-optimized retirement plan? They're walking around with insurance policies that would cover maybe two years of their lifestyle if something happened to them. When I ask them about their coverage, they often proudly mention that their employer provides life insurance equal to twice their annual salary—as if replacing just two years of income is sufficient when they have twenty more earning years ahead of them!

In this chapter, I'm going to challenge your assumptions about what "adequate insurance coverage" really means for someone with our typical client profile. Let's get this out of the way upfront: It's probably a lot more than you currently have.

Before I start discussing insurance with you all, I want to explain how my firm handles insurance so you can understand our biases, potential conflicts of interest, and the like. As part of our comprehensive planning approach, we review our clients' insurance needs: analyzing their coverage, determining gaps/opportunities, and then, if they need additional coverage, our insurance team will go out and procure it for them.

So, yes, we sell life insurance when our clients need it. That said, less than 0.5% (meaning half of 1%) of our firm's annual revenue comes from insurance, and over 95% of the policies we do implement are inexpensive term insurance policies that pay us very little.

Simply put, it would be easier and more economical for our firm to NOT get involved in insurance, but we don't think ignoring a major part of a client's plan or passing it off to a random third party is in our clients' best interests.

Now, back to the matter at hand.

There is one planning gap that I see relentlessly and repeatedly from our clients: Even those clients who are doing everything else right and have a 95+% chance of success in their long-term plan do not have enough term life insurance. We'll get into why that's the case in a moment, but let's start with the basics: a life insurance explainer.

Fundamentally, there are two types of insurance:

- Term life insurance
- Permanent life insurance

For the purposes of this chapter, we will focus on "term" life insurance, but you can read more about permanent life insurance in Chapter 31. "Term' life insurance is life insurance that you purchase for a specific and limited period.

So, if you buy a twenty-year term insurance policy with a $1M death benefit, and you pass away at any point during that twenty-year period, your beneficiary will receive $1M tax-free. But if you pass away in year twenty-two, when you no longer have the insurance coverage (and are no longer paying the insurance premiums, naturally), they will receive nothing. It is insurance in its purest form: There is no cash build-up or savings component. If you outlive the term period you've chosen, you do not receive any money back (which, obviously, is the best-case scenario as it means you're still alive!). One relevant note: Throughout the life of your term policy, you have the option to convert the coverage to the permanent type, if you so choose. This means that if you do decide that you want coverage for life, you can always make that pivot

Because of this limited form of protection, term insurance coverage is inexpensive relative to other, permanent types of insurance—that is its best attribute (and in a lot of cases, the only one we need!). Most people can (and should) be able to buy the amount of term life insurance they need to protect their family without breaking their budget.

Now that we've covered the basics, let's examine the problem of underinsurance, since we see it time and time again. When do we see the biggest insurance gaps with our clients?

Let's dive in:

1. **You have (or will soon have) a young and/or growing family.** In this case, getting $2M or $5M of *permanent* life insurance isn't practical. It would be too expensive, complicated, and just downright unnecessary

for most young families. At this stage of life, we are fundamentally concerned with protecting your family for the next twenty years (i.e., your working and childcare years). As you get older and your net worth grows (and the kids move out of the house), you will have less of a need for quite as much death benefit protection as when you were young—a phase of life where you had less money AND more family responsibilities. Term insurance, therefore, fills the insurance need for the specific period that you are most vulnerable and in most need of the largest amount of family protection.

2. **You have a mortgage and student loans.** Most people, when buying a home and getting a mortgage, look to get term insurance to cover the outstanding mortgage balance so that, if something were to happen to them, their family could easily pay off the mortgage. While this is obviously smart thinking, it typically understates how much income your family would need to replace if you passed away prematurely! The mortgage is obviously the biggest ticket item, but putting that aside, they will still have their bills, the kids' college tuition(s), vacation(s), retirement, etc., all without thirty years of your income contributing to the mix.

3. **You are responsible for older family members.** If you know that one day it will be your responsibility to

care for your elderly parents, uncle, grandma, etc., we want to make sure that even if you pass away before accumulating the funds you'll need to take care of them, they will still be protected and financially supported.

Those are three of the most common scenarios in which we see people underprepared in case the worst happens—and the reasons why term insurance would make sense for them.

Even if none of those reasons convinced you, maybe this one will: If you run a simple cost-benefit analysis on getting term insurance, the answer is emphatic: *Why not?* Because term insurance is both inexpensive and based on your age and health (meaning, the younger and healthier you are, the lower the cost of the coverage), it is worthwhile to set it up (in some amount) once you start making a significant income, even if you don't have an immediate need or aren't sure of how much to get. I truly believe that. Money affords you freedom, opportunity, and security. For the price of two cocktails per month, you can ensure that the people closest to you are in a better financial position if you were to pass away. And once you have the policy, you never have to worry about something happening to you that might prevent you from getting insurance in the future (like getting sick, injured, etc.), as you at least have this policy locked in for twenty to thirty years. Here's one example: A $2M, thirty-year term policy for a healthy forty-year-old female would cost approximately $1,500 per year. PER YEAR. This is a rounding error in your spending habits, while the potential benefit to your family (if, God forbid, you passed away prematurely) might be life-changing.

I personally have a $2M, twenty-year term policy, and I set it up when I was not married, didn't own a home, and didn't have kids. (Side note: I wrote parts of this book when I was dating my now-wife, parts when I was engaged, and am now wrapping up after getting married . . . writing about my stage of life throughout this book is a bit confusing. Bear with me!)

Why'd I get the insurance? Because I could! I now have this coverage for the next twenty years, and my family is immediately covered if something were to happen to me. Of course, when I do have kids, I'll get more coverage as my needs will have increased—but what if in three years I get sick and I'm not able to get this additional coverage? It gives me peace of mind to know that even in this worst-case scenario, I at least have $2M of term insurance already on the books to protect my family.

A quick note . . . I'm not counting the life insurance you likely have through your employer as part of your family's ongoing protection plan. It's great that you have it, and you should absolutely continue to elect this coverage the next time enrollment opens. Ultimately, however, it's not a recipe for true family protection, because if/when you leave your job, you will no longer have the coverage. What if you change jobs and your new company doesn't have life insurance coverage? What if you move to a startup? What if you take time off in the future or start your own business? There are too many variables to rely on consistently over the next twenty to thirty years to depend on non-portable coverage.

Let's use an example as a prompt for thinking about the amount of coverage that makes sense for your family. Let's say you make $350K and your spouse makes $200K. Your household income is $550K.

Here are the relevant questions to determine your insurance needs:

- How much of my income do I want to replace if I pass away?
- How much of that $350K would my spouse need each year to pay the bills and get the kids through school?

Let's assume you have a $2M term insurance policy. This means that if you pass away, your spouse will receive $2M tax-free. If they then invest the $2M in an income-oriented portfolio, they would be able to withdraw 4% in interest each year (since interest is the amount of money you can withdraw without liquidating any principal).

This would provide $80K in income per year, without touching the $2M itself.

You might be wondering why we're assuming that you wouldn't draw down the $2M principal as part of this plan. We could, but I'd rather be cautious when it comes to family protection, because it's not just about covering your living expenses for the next few years. We need to worry about paying for your kids' future college tuition (not to mention summer camp for your youngest and tennis lessons for your oldest), one or two weddings you'd like to pay for, grad school, etc. It's morbid, but the costs you expected your income to cover would now need to be paid without it!

Think about this, too: If your spouse passes away in the near term, you'd be losing out on another twenty to thirty years of *retirement contributions* that you'll no longer be able to make either.

Simply put, we want to generate enough income from the death benefit proceeds to live on NOW during your working years, while your kids are growing up so we can leave the principal ($2M) to grow and support retirement, housing, health care, education, and other large one-off expenses to come.

If you are making enough money to save $5K or $15K per month (and all our clients fall somewhere in that range), then yes! You absolutely should spend $1–4K per year to protect your family in case it all goes wrong over the next thirty years! The cost-benefit analysis—the minimal cost now compared to how life-changing the coverage could be for your family—makes this a no-brainer.

Now that we've addressed protecting your family with adequate life insurance, let's talk about protecting something equally important but often overlooked: your ability to earn an income in the first place.

23

Disability Insurance: Your Income Is Your Greatest Asset—Is It Protected?

"There are things in life worse than death. Have you ever spent an evening with an insurance salesman?"
–Woody Allen

When I asked Oliver, a new client and a brilliant tech executive, what his most valuable asset was, he practically beamed. "Oh, it's definitely my investment portfolio," he said proudly, then joked, "Though my World War Two book collection is a close second." I hate to say it, but Oliver was wrong. Not just about the books—but about his portfolio. He was missing what was right in front of him.

If you're a high-earning professional in your late thirties or forties, your greatest asset is the financial engine that powers everything else: your ability to earn an income for the next twenty-plus years. Think about it. If you make $400K annually, your future earnings over the next two decades represent an $8M asset. That's likely more than everything else on your balance sheet combined!

Yet most professionals I meet have barely given a thought to what would happen if that income stream were suddenly interrupted by illness or injury. Here's a question for you: If your $3M home had inadequate insurance coverage, you'd fix that immediately, right? It's just one of those things you know to take care of. So why would you leave an $8M asset exposed?

Most W-2 professionals have disability insurance as part of their group plan at work, and this is a wonderful thing, but it may not be enough to adequately protect you and your family if you were to get injured or fall sick. Here are a few things to keep in mind as you look through the long-term disability package you get through work (or if you have a financial advisor, here's what they should be keeping in mind as they scroll through these documents):

- Does your work policy have a coverage limit? I have seen plenty of group disability policies that pay up to a monthly maximum of $10K or $15K. If you make $500K per year and your lifestyle is dependent on you continuing to make that income, well, only having $120K come in from your group (employer) disability policy isn't going to cut it. It would be worth exploring your ability to fill in the gaps with an individually owned, long-term disability policy that you buy outside of work.

- Are the benefits taxable? If your company pays for your disability insurance coverage—you'll be able to see if this is the case on your pay stub—then the benefits (if you ever need them) will be taxable as ordinary income. This can further reduce the amount of income you actually receive from your group policy. A personal policy that you pay for will be tax-free if you use the insurance. To that end, if given the option by your employer to pay for your group long-term disability policy as opposed to letting your employer pay for it—you should seriously consider paying yourself! If you pay the premiums, the benefits will be tax-free if you unfortunately do end up needing to use the disability insurance.

I would MUCH rather pay taxes on the income/ money I use to pay the premiums than pay taxes on the insurance income if it ends up paying out. For one, the premiums are likely much smaller than the potential disability income benefits, so the total amount of tax on the premiums is also (naturally) much lower. And secondly, and far more importantly, when would you rather worry about taxes: when you're healthy and earning a lot of money OR when you're disabled and more stressed about money than you've ever been?

- You want to make sure you specify "own occupation" in your disability policy. This means that the policy will pay out if you are unable to perform the specific responsibilities of the *specific job* you are paid for. For a common example of why this matters, imagine a surgeon's situation. They may be injured to the point that they're unable to perform surgeries (for instance, if something happens to their hands, or they can't stand for eight-plus hours), but they could still teach or consult based on their knowledge and experience. A disability insurance policy that was defined as "any occupation" would not pay out under those circumstances, even though they might now be making $100K per year rather than the $800K they were paid as a surgeon.

I've intentionally kept this chapter on disability insurance short. We could get into the weeds of different riders and benefits, but quite frankly, all of those need to be discussed and walked through on an individual basis. The important takeaway is this: If you make north of $350K+, you should dedicate time to understanding how protected you are through your group coverage at work and whether there are any gaps to address. One in four professionals will need disability insurance at some point in their careers. This is not an area to ignore, nor where you should pinch pennies!

We've covered protecting your income during your lifetime, but what about afterward? Not to go too dark, but we all know it's true: Proper financial planning also means considering what happens to your assets when you're no longer here to manage them.

24

Estate Plans: You Have One
(It Was Either Created by You or the Government)

"The correct lesson to learn from surprises is that the world is surprising. Not that we should use past surprises as a guide to future boundaries; that we should use past surprises as an admission that we have no idea what might happen next."
— Morgan Housel

I'll let you in on a little secret that most people don't realize until it's too late: You already have an estate plan.

Yes, you.

Even if you've never set foot in an attorney's office or signed a single estate document, the question isn't whether you have a plan; it's whether you created that plan yourself or are defaulting to the one the government has created for you. It's like showing up to a costume party—you're either wearing the outfit you carefully selected, or you're stuck with whatever random getup the host assigns to those who didn't bring their own. And trust me, the government's "default costume" for your estate rarely matches what you would have chosen for yourself.

The good news? Taking control of your estate plan is far less complicated, time-consuming, and expensive than most people imagine. Let's walk through what you need to know. When it comes to proactive estate planning, I'll start here: Estate planning is not just for the already "super" wealthy.

That's like saying you shouldn't open a 401(k), a high-yield savings account, or evaluate your cash flow and budget until you're already super wealthy.

For one, it won't be easy to become super wealthy unless you start doing some of those things. And two, this totally misses the point: Foundational estate planning documents aren't even about your assets!

Broadly speaking, there are two functions of estate planning. We'll get to the second at the end of this chapter. The first is simply the act of organizing your affairs for when you are incapacitated, unavailable, or have passed away (and even within this one estate planning area, we find that people only ever think of estate planning as pertaining to the last one, when the first two are statistically much more likely).

Whether you have $100K or $10M to your name, you should have certain foundational documents (such as a will or trust, a health-care proxy, and durable power of attorney) so that you have a plan in place if you can't (for whatever reason) continue to manage your affairs on your own.

To use just one example: Avoiding probate (a public court process that can be lengthy and expensive in some states) might be an important estate planning goal for your family. I certainly recommend avoiding the probate process if possible!

Well, I've heard dozens of clients come to us saying they have a will and therefore are all set. While setting up a will is better than dying without one (which is called "dying intestate"), it doesn't help you avoid probate! In fact, even if you die with a will, your assets will still go through the public probate process, and it can take months or even years before your family receives them. (Unsurprisingly, California is a state that has an unbearably long probate process.)

So, what's the alternative? Setting up a revocable trust and using a trust-based estate plan as an alternative to a will can serve to avoid the cumbersome probate process entirely.

To "nerd out" for a moment: A revocable trust is simply a trust agreement where you, as the "trustor" or "grantor," have the ability to amend or revoke the trust at any time (including terminating the trust if you wanted to), and from which you can deposit and withdraw assets as you see fit. You can specify in the trust agreement who controls the trust (the "trustee") and who gets the benefit of the assets in the trust (the "beneficiary"), and *you* can play both roles while you're alive! I say all this simply to emphasize that it's not the type of "trust" most people think of, where you're giving away money or avoiding estate taxes or anything like that. A *revocable* trust does nothing for tax purposes because it's still your asset . . . it's just owned in a trust you control!

Again, the point of the revocable trust is that it accomplishes the same objectives as a will (i.e., naming your beneficiaries and how your assets will be distributed when you pass away) while also avoiding probate and privatizing the process (since, unlike a will, the details of your trust are not something anyone can just look up online!). A trust is also legally binding as soon as you put something in it, whereas a will only takes effect at death, so the trust also provides value to you if you are incapacitated before you pass away.

Obviously, this is a very high-level and superficial introduction to revocable trusts and wills. My point is not to be definitive here (and it's certainly NOT TO PROVIDE LEGAL ADVICE—please consult an attorney!) but rather to highlight how being proactive and intentional with your planning can avoid headaches later—for you *and* your family.

Anecdotally, I can say this is one of the areas where clients need the most help and have gotten the least done before we start working together. We've seen a number of prospective clients who make $500K+, have kids approaching elementary school age, are maxing out retirement accounts, and have personal life insurance, but mention that estate planning is still "on their to-do list." *Your kids are five and eight . . . you haven't updated your estate plan since they were born?!*

Of course, I understand why this is so common and I NEVER judge them for it. Estate planning is scary and forces us to confront our own mortality. It makes parents ask themselves an even more overwhelming question: *What if I'm not here to take care of my kids?* I've also found that sometimes parents kick the can down the road when it comes to naming guardians for their kids because they can't imagine anyone taking better care of their kids than they could. While I'm sure this is true, we still want to make that decision ourselves rather than leave it up to chance.

Estate planning has also historically been expensive and time-consuming, and forces you to interact with attorneys you've never met before, who don't know you and your family, and in whose presence, you always feel "on the clock." (Again . . . saying it all out loud, I really do get the hesitation!)

Because of all this friction, some of the elements of our planning process that I'm proudest of are our firm's partnership with a powerful estate planning platform and our hiring of an in-house estate planning specialist who's there specifically to solve this gap that SO many people come to us with. With this setup, we can provide our clients with the means to create well-executed estate planning documents—and in a cost-effective way.

So that's the first function of estate planning. What's the second? Transferring your wealth in a tax-smart way while considering federal and state estate tax laws. (A lot of people think this is the ONLY function of estate planning, and therefore it's something only the super wealthy should do—but as I hope you realize after reading this chapter, that is a misconception.)

Diving any deeper into this second motivation is beyond the scope of this book, so I'll just say that if you are a high-income-earning family in your thirties or forties, planning for the estate tax might be something you need to think about sooner than you realize.

Now that we've covered protecting your assets and begun discussing how to transfer them according to your wishes, it's time to dig into smart strategies for maximizing what you keep in the first place.

25

Tax Compliance vs. Tax Advice vs. Tax Planning ... We Want All Three!

"The art of taxation consists in so plucking the goose as to obtain the largest amount of feathers with the least amount of hissing."

– Jean-Baptiste Colbert

There's a fundamental misunderstanding that costs high earners thousands—sometimes hundreds of thousands—over their lifetimes. It's the belief that filing your taxes correctly each April means you're handling your tax situation optimally.

One has very little to do with the other.

What most people do is tax compliance, not tax planning. And in my mind, tax planning is a very specific thing.

In this chapter, I'll show you why your relationship with your CPA might not be delivering the value you think it is, and how shifting from an annual tax mindset to a lifetime tax strategy can transform your financial future.

So, what do I mean when I say that, in my mind, tax planning is a very specific thing?

You are engaged in tax planning if you have a philosophy and a strategy designed to pay the least amount of taxes possible over your lifespan.

I'll say that again, because most people don't think about paying the least amount in taxes over their entire life. They think (and have been conditioned to think) that the goal should be to pay the least amount of taxes in each individual year. Right? I mean, think about last tax season—wasn't your instinct to find ways to lower your tax bill for that year? I get it, of course, it's natural! But it's also shortsighted. It's the tax version of winning the battle but losing the war.

I'll say it plainly: Attempting to pay the least amount in taxes each year, without any consideration of what effect this will have on your FUTURE tax liability, is a recipe for overpaying the IRS over the course of your lifetime. Instead, effective tax planning forces you to think about how this year's tax bill will impact next year's, which can impact five years from now, which will impact your tax bill in retirement, and so on.

You have to think about your taxes as an evolving, multi-year process in which you are adding and removing income to your "tax bucket" based on how much you will pay in taxes as a result (i.e., based on your marginal tax bracket).

In my experience, taxes are the part of the planning process around which there is the most confusion and the least clarity on what constitutes "having a plan."

I also think far too many people believe they're engaged in tax planning when they're just engaged in a more basic (but still super important) function like tax compliance or tax "advice"—both things you do while working with a tax preparer (like a CPA or enrolled agent) within a single tax year. Both are important, but neither constitutes real tax planning. So, with that in mind, let's break down the three stages of tax awareness—compliance, advice, and planning—and what they each entail.

Imagine these three concepts diagramed like one of those food pyramids we all studied in school: tax compliance at the bottom (everyone who files their taxes does this in some manner), followed by tax advice (not as common), and finally, tax planning (even less common, but holding the top spot of the pyramid!). Except in this case, the importance is reversed: back in school, the top of the pyramid was for the stuff to eat the least, but here, you want to spend the MOST amount of time and focus at the top of the pyramid, on tax planning.

1. Tax Compliance

This is the baseline: filing your tax return and paying the appropriate amount of tax based on your adjusted gross income, marginal tax bracket, and relevant deductions. You are making sure you are compliant with the IRS for that given tax year. A tax preparer (CPA or enrolled agent) can get this done for you and will typically leave the picture at the end of tax season once your filing is complete. In this way, tax preparation is reactive—almost by definition! You are handing your tax preparer all your relevant documents (e.g., W-2, 1099 self-employment income, 1099-R investment statements, pay stubs, and family status), and they are simply taking that information and ensuring it is processed accurately on your tax return.

(A quick note: Getting a tax refund should not be cause for celebration and does not mean your tax preparer did a "good job." This just means you overpaid the IRS throughout the year and gave them a zero-interest loan, rather than you getting to hold onto that money and allocate it as you see fit.)

If the only time you speak to your CPA is around tax time . . . well, then you have a tax preparer and you are not, in any way, engaged in a tax-planning relationship, because tax planning happens throughout the entire year. There's not much planning you can do if you (and your CPA) have no idea what's happening in your tax world until you collect the documents a month before the tax deadline.

Now, to be clear, I absolutely believe that tax preparation is a valuable service! Heck, Drucker Wealth offers tax prep services to our ongoing wealth management clients! And if you're thinking about whether to do your own tax returns or hire a tax preparer to file them for you . . . I strongly believe you should hire a tax preparer. Tax compliance is way too important to leave anything up to chance. If you do your own taxes, you're filing one return per year and hoping you did it right. A tax preparer does hundreds of returns each year and knows what they're looking for.

My perspective is that if you make $300K+ per year and you're not willing to pay $500–$1,500 per year to get your taxes done, your sense of value and pricing needs updating. The time you save on dealing with your tax return is worth a whole lot more than $1K annually!

A few examples of what a tax preparer might find:

- You're taking the standard deduction when you really should be itemizing based on your mortgage interest, state taxes, and charitable contributions.
- You made a backdoor Roth contribution and need to file Form 8606 to report it to the IRS.

- You didn't take the qualified business income (QBI) deduction even though you were eligible.
- You made contributions to an HSA but didn't remember to include those as an above-the-line deduction.

2. Tax Advice

I'm defining this as when your tax preparer also gives you advice as to how to lower your tax bill on your current tax return. A proactive tax preparer will be helpful in this way. Rather than just inputting the numbers and filing your tax return, they will think through the return and offer strategies, tips, and suggestions for you to pay less in tax . . . cool!

So why do I not consider this tax planning?

Because if you are only looking at each tax year in isolation, you're not actually devising a strategy that will mean paying less in taxes over your lifetime. In fact, paying the least amount in taxes each year just about guarantees that, at some point in the future, you will pay a lot more in taxes! The secret to understanding the tax code is knowing that all income will be taxed at some point. Choosing to take a deduction today means adding taxable income later, and foregoing a deduction today (i.e., choosing to pay the tax) might mean less tax later.

Just to be clear: The CPA is not doing anything wrong by trying to minimize your tax bill each year. They are hired, in most cases, on a year-by-year basis to help you file your taxes and are conditioned to help you pay the least amount of taxes while they're working with you . . . they're doing their job! Most taxpayers don't think about their lifetime tax bill and so judge their tax preparer by how much tax they ended up paying that year and whether the preparer "saved them any money in taxes"—for that year only.

So, what's the alternative?

3. Tax Planning

Effective tax planning is about using your marginal tax bracket to your advantage and controlling when you pay taxes based on how much tax you would pay for the same deduction in different years.

In the years when you are in a lower tax bracket, we want to add more taxable income to your bucket, and in the years when you are in a higher tax bracket and already have a lot of income, we want to find ways to take income out. We want to maximize how much each tax deduction actually benefits you in the year that you take it!

Paying the least amount possible in taxes *each year* (which means only looking at taxes on an individual-year basis) prevents you from doing this. Let's consider an example. Imagine that this year, you are taking some time off work and, as a result, are only in the 12% tax bracket. Your tax preparer tells you that you can add an additional $5K to your pre-tax 401(k) to lower your tax bill, and you think, *Great, I'm lowering my tax bill . . . sign me up!* But if you wanted to look at lowering your *lifetime* tax bill, you would think about the opportunity differently.

Instead, you might think, *Well, right now I'm only in the 12% tax bracket. This is the lowest tax bracket I'm probably ever going to be in. Why would I want to further lower this year's taxable income, when doing so would only save me twelve cents on the dollar? In fact, I want to go the other way: I want to fill up the 12% tax bucket to the very top (without going into the 24% tax bracket). Given that, not only should I put $5K more into my Roth 401(k) and forego the tax savings this year so I can benefit in retirement, but I am actually going to convert my $10K Rollover IRA into a Roth, pay the 12% income tax . . . and then I'll have all of this money to take out income-tax-free when I go back up and am paying taxes at a higher bracket.*

So, again, looking at each year in isolation would have you taking a 12% tax deduction TODAY instead of considering a multi-year strategy that would lower your taxable income in a year when you are in a much higher tax bracket.

A few additional points to bear in mind:

1. You should stop thinking about taxes as a "season"—"I'm getting organized for tax season"—and think of them more as an ongoing conversation to be had throughout the year.

2. A tax preparer (CPA/enrolled agent) is a great start, but they should be paired with a proactive financial planner who looks at what your tax bill will look like at different stages of your life and plans accordingly.

3. An investment strategy is not isolated from a tax strategy. Taxes have an impact on every aspect of

investment management (via tax loss/gain harvesting, tax-sensitive asset allocation, Roth conversions, cash flow opportunities, employer retirement options, etc.).

4. Estate planning and risk management are not isolated from tax strategy. Decisions you make about how to protect your assets and income can go a long way toward lowering your lifetime tax bill (e.g., taxable versus tax-free disability insurance planning, using trusts to keep assets out of your taxable estate, maximizing the tax benefits of your charitable giving, or being aware of gift/estate tax limits).

We'll have more to say about specific tax strategies in the next section, but in the meantime, think about how you've handled your taxes in the last few years. Have you mostly just been thinking about taxes seasonally? Have you been reviewing your tax returns each year looking for planning opportunities? Hopefully, no matter how you answer, you're motivated to take action!

In this section, we've dismantled the dangerous myths that keep high earners financially stuck. You now understand the crucial distinction between volatility and risk, why your home isn't the investment everyone claims it is, the truth about risk management, and why trying to outsmart the market with individual stock picks is a fool's errand for even the aspiring Warren Buffetts among us.

These aren't just abstract concepts—they're the practical foundations that will completely transform how you approach your wealth. More than anything, when taken together, they're a plea to think about your money and financial decision-making process in an intentional and proactive way. It doesn't even matter whether you agree with each individual concept. Maybe you still want to buy rental property, or you still consider yourself a "conservative investor" even in the context that we've laid out . . . that's fine! We have GREAT clients who do both! But making those decisions after considering the context and opportunity costs is different from defaulting to these positions!

And, as we move on to the next section, I'll emphasize that understanding these philosophies is only half the journey. Knowledge without implementation is just trivia—interesting at cocktail parties, but useless for building real wealth.

That's why in Part 3, we're rolling up our sleeves and diving into the tactical playbook that will turn these philosophies into tangible results. I'll share specific approaches to tax loss harvesting and Roth conversions that could save you thousands in taxes. You'll learn how to maximize 529 plans and other education-funding vehicles for your children. You'll gain clarity on RSUs and equity compensation, business structures, and estate planning essentials that most advisors rarely explain clearly. These are the exact dynamic techniques my team and I use every day with our clients, yielding consistently impactful results.

That's what I want for you, too.

The difference between those who merely earn well and those who build lasting wealth isn't intelligence or luck—it's the disciplined application of sound principles followed by decisive action.

Congrats—you've uncovered the principles to rewrite your financial reality. Now let's put them to work.

PART 3
SPECIFIC AND TACTICAL PLANNING SITUATIONS

"Dear IRS, I am writing to you to cancel my subscription. Please remove my name from your mailing list."
–Snoopy (as a character in *Peanuts*)

BEHAVIOR GAP

This section is all about the details: What are the most common strategies and tactics that we implement on a day-to-day basis to help our clients maximize their financial situation?

When clients and I begin working together, we typically need six to eight Zoom meetings to walk through their financial program. That might sound like a lot, but we're dealing with a lot: cash flow, investing, taxes, estate planning, insurance, and goal planning! When setting the stage for these conversations, I explain that we will start at a high level (helicopter view) and get progressively deeper into the details as we move through. We need to answer the big questions, like, "How do we balance our intention to send the kids to private school with buying a new house?" or "Are we on the right track to be work optional by fifty-five?" and "Does our saving capacity match our actual cash flow over the last six months?" before we laser in on specific tactics like, "We need to eliminate some redundant investment funds in your brokerage account" or "You should sign up for your after-tax 401(k) and complete a mega backdoor Roth."

I view this book the same way.

Part 1 gave you a more complete understanding of what real financial planning is and who can benefit from it. Whether you choose to find a financial partner or do it on your own, I hope your takeaway is that your age and net worth should not be deterrents from building an intentional and comprehensive financial plan.

Part 2 aimed to provide you with the confidence and knowledge to build your financial foundation from the ground up, focusing on (what I consider) the building blocks of any solid financial plan. Whether you agreed with everything I wrote or not is immaterial; I hope it provided food for thought and will help you dig deeper.

In Part 3, I will outline the tactical steps you can take to start making intentional financial decisions moving forward.

These next chapters will cover a wide range of areas. I've grouped the concepts as best I can: tax strategies first, funding your children's goals second, and equity compensation third.

But while it's helpful to understand the whole, and while I will continuously try to bring it all together, these chapters are the most "stand-alone" in the book, in the sense that you can cherry-pick the ones most relevant to your financial day-to-day. As you continue to progress in your career, you can also revisit this section to determine whether these strategies make sense for you down the road.

Before we move on to the details, I want to leave you with one hard-hitting truth: Financial literacy in America (even among high earners) isn't great. I believe this is due to gaps in both behavior and knowledge.

I've already tried to help you reckon with the behavioral gap. Now it's time to tackle the knowledge gap. You'll be unsurprised to discover that I firmly believe this one is both easier to solve and not, ultimately, as important to your overall success as is your financial behavior—which is why we're starting this section 229 pages in.

Nevertheless, the story is incomplete without the sort of strategies and tactics that will directly and meaningfully improve your financial outcomes—so that's where we turn next!

26

Tax Loss Harvesting

"The hardest thing in the world to understand is the income tax."
–Albert Einstein

The idea of writing a second book came to me as 2022 was winding down, but I did most of my writing in 2023 and 2024 and finished the book in 2025. Those are some illustrative years for understanding the value of tax loss harvesting!

Let's start with 2022. The stock market (using the S&P 500 as a stand-in for the market as a whole) lost 19% in 2022. It was the first down year in a long time, and the worst year in the stock market since 2008. As we addressed in Part 2, all of this was—and is—of no concern for the long-term investor.

I'm emphasizing this downturn only because 2022's market decline provided us all with an opportunity to harvest our investment losses as part of a strategy to lower our adjusted gross income (AGI) for the year.

Do you remember if you did this? Did you report $3K in capital losses in 2022? (Check your tax return!) More importantly, do you remember thinking about these tax opportunities popping up throughout the year? Were you aware of them?

Every situation is different, and maybe you didn't want to take tax losses for a particular reason, but that's kind of my point. I hope it was a conscious decision either way. If not, then I would absolutely reevaluate your investment process moving forward. Are you paying enough attention to the tax consequences of your investment program?

With that as a preamble, let's dive into what tax loss harvesting looks like in practice.

We'll start with the basics.

Every year, during tax time, your CPA will have to report any capital gains or capital losses that you've realized across all your taxable investment portfolios during the prior year (this is done via a tax document called "1099-B").

A capital event (gain or loss) occurs anytime you've sold any of the holdings inside your portfolio during the year (for mutual funds, there's an extra level of nuance because they pay out all gains throughout the year, but the concept remains the same).

The tax ramifications for these gains and losses depend on how long you've held each individual position in your portfolio. If you held the security for at least twelve months and one day, any gains you realize will be treated as a long-term gain or loss. You will be taxed at a more preferential rate (15% or 20%, for most of our clients) on those gains compared to the taxes you pay on earned income (i.e., your W-2 or self-employment income) throughout the year (which comes in at 32% or 37% for most of our clients).

Alternatively, if you've held the security (e.g., stock, ETFs, and index funds) for less than a year, then the capital gain will be treated as a short-term gain, which has the same tax treatment as ordinary income as described above.

So, for example, if you have a taxable long-term capital gain of $5K from selling a stock in portfolio A and $3K of capital losses from selling a stock in portfolio B, when looked at together, you will have a total of $2K of long-term gains. This $2K will be reportable on your return, and, assuming a 20% long-term capital gain rate, you will owe $400. (And yes, we are ignoring Net Investment Income Tax in order to emphasize a single variable, but of course, it might be relevant for you! For additional details of how capital gains and losses are netted, see IRS publication 550.)

An important distinction to make is that this only applies to "realized" capital gains and losses. If you bought ten shares of Amazon stock in 2012 and never sold a share, well, you've never actually "realized" any capital gains because you haven't yet materially profited from those shares. The gains are still sitting inside the portfolio, unrealized. You will ultimately pay the tax gains on the increase in Amazon's value whenever you do sell the shares.

If you have net realized capital losses—meaning that among all of your realized (sold) investment gains and investment losses throughout the year, you ultimately have more losses than gains—you'll be able to use those losses to lower your ordinary income tax liability for the year. The maximum amount of loss you can use against your ordinary income is $3K annually, and the rest gets pushed into future tax years. (See IRS Publication 550 for more details.)

Example: Let's assume that this year, you have $5K of capital gains in your accounts and $9K of capital losses. This means you have net losses of $4K. You can use $3K of those losses to offset ordinary income tax in the current year (amazing!), and the remaining $1K can offset capital gains in the following year.

By the way, proactively realizing tax losses isn't a strategy to be used exclusively during years, like 2022, when the market loses money. We can (and should!) do so in any market environment. To illustrate: In 2025, a year that, at least as I edit here, is on track for double-digit positive returns, we were STILL able to proactively harvest meaningful tax losses in most of our clients' accounts. Because the market lost money so quickly in April and then spent the next six months rising higher, we were able to aggressively harvest tax losses during that rough three-week period, while enjoying the market returns that followed!

In the accounts we manage, we are always looking for opportunities to harvest losses where possible. When the markets lose money for any period of time, and losses materialize all around us, that is fertile ground to begin tax loss harvesting!

To do so, we will sell positions that are operating at a loss and buy a "secondary" holding (a similar holding that takes the same general investment approach we just sold). We will hold this "secondary" holding for thirty-one days to avoid the wash sale rule, and then buy back the original holding we had built the portfolio strategy around. Every step of this multifaceted approach is important. The benefits are twofold:

1. Harvesting the loss (by selling the position) allows you to lower your tax liability and effective tax rate in the current year. As they say, lemonade from lemons.

2. Because we are buying a "secondary" fund, we are not just sitting on the sidelines (sitting in cash) for the thirty-one days we are waiting to buy back your portfolio. If the market rebounds over that thirty-one-day period, we remain fully invested and will still be materially participating in the positive returns the market begins providing.

At Drucker Wealth, because our clients are in such a high tax bracket and because tax loss harvesting saves real money come tax time, we like utilizing strategies that increase our ability to harvest tax loss year-to-year. To this end, we frequently invest using custom index portfolios—taxable accounts in which we unwrap the index of whatever asset class we're investing in and instead buy the underlying stocks that make up that index. So, if our strategy calls for owning the S&P 500 (large cap stocks) instead of owning an S&P 500 ETF, we might buy the underlying 500 companies that make up the S&P 500 instead. Doing so allows us to tax loss harvest at the individual security level, rather than only being able to do so if the entire asset (large cap stocks) loses money. At any given point, the asset class might have positive returns, but there will usually be a number of individual companies within the asset class that have lost money and can therefore be sold and replaced. For example, in 2023, the stock market averaged over 25% for the year, even as 1,085 companies in the Russell 3000 Index lost money![27]

A point worth making here: This is still a passive investment strategy. Even though we own individual stocks in a custom indexing account, we are not actually "picking" which stocks to own, like one would in an active strategy. The goal is to match the risk parameters and the performance of the underlying index.

That's probably enough about tax loss harvesting for now. We'll touch on a second benefit of using custom indexing accounts—investing around concentrated positions—in an upcoming chapter on receiving RSUs and strategizing around company stock (Chapter 34).

The flip side of tax loss harvesting is tax gain harvesting, which is just as effective a strategy (though it tends to be less common with our clients simply because of their stage of life and their high incomes). Capital gain harvesting is when you're in a particularly low tax bracket for a given year (maybe you took a sabbatical, left your job, and took a while to find the next role, or something similar). It therefore makes sense to sell positions you've been holding for a while so that the resultant capital gains fill up the zero percent bracket first.

If you have a position with thousands of dollars of capital gains that you haven't wanted to pay taxes on, and you sell now, all you've done is fill the zero percent tax bracket to the top—and zero percent of anything is ZERO! If, however, you wait and sell that stock when you're back up to the 15% capital gains bracket, now you're paying 15% tax on all those gains. This is why tax-aware investing is so important: It's the same amount of real gain, but a totally different tax treatment depending on the year you sell!

To be clear, tax loss and gain harvesting needs to be done with an efficient, managed approach that avoids wash sale rules and aggregation rules between accounts, and with an awareness of your tax bracket. It should only be done with a CFP® or tax advisor. But if you are not at least exploring how tax loss harvesting during down markets can affect your overall tax planning, you're missing out.

27

Backdoor Roths and Roth Conversion Planning

"Taxes: Of life's two certainties, the only one for which you can get an automatic extension."
—Anonymous

Winston Churchill once said, "Never let a good crisis go to waste."

Okay, fine, our topic isn't as dramatic or important as anything Mr. Churchill was dealing with. But the same truth applies: When the markets go down, there are opportunities to make lemonade out of lemons (tax savings out of lower share prices, but tomato/tomahto).

We discussed one of these opportunities—tax loss harvesting—in the last chapter. Later in this chapter, we're going to discuss another: the market-driven Roth IRA conversion. But first, to set the stage, let's spend some time discussing the tax implications of the various ways to save for retirement.

Many of you have 401(k)s and 403(b)s through your employer. You can allocate your contributions entirely to the traditional 401(k), entirely to the Roth, or some combination of both. The difference is simply when you're choosing to pay taxes on the money.

With a traditional or pre-tax 401(k), IRA, 403(b)—or SEP IRA/solo 401(k) if you're self-employed—you don't pay federal taxes on your contribution in the current year. The funds grow tax-deferred over time, but you will pay ordinary income tax whenever you distribute the money in retirement.

Let's not overlook this last piece.

Say you have $1M in your 401(k) and you want to liquidate the portfolio at sixty-two to buy a vacation home.

You're only actually going to net about $600K to $700K (assuming a 30% tax bracket), because every dollar you take out is immediately taxable at ordinary income rates. And this makes sense: You've never paid a dollar in taxes on the money in that account. Not when you contributed the funds and not as it grew.

With a Roth IRA/401(k), it's the opposite. Your contribution does not result in a tax deduction in the current year, but the money will grow tax-free and be distributed tax-free in retirement. So, if you have $1M inside your Roth IRA, you will net the full $1M when you decide to distribute the funds. You do not owe the IRS any portion of your retirement account.

This is why we consistently talk with clients about the fact that the value of their money is not simply reflected by the number on their statement. In this example, the difference between having $1M in your pre-tax account and $1M in your Roth is hundreds of thousands of dollars when it comes to your ability to spend that money!

Roth accounts are also a lot more flexible once you start taking money out in retirement, because unlike pre-tax retirement accounts, they don't have Required Minimum Distributions (RMDs). RMDs are distributions that you are government-mandated to start taking once you reach a certain age (it used to be seventy and a half; now it's either seventy-two, seventy-three, or seventy-five, depending on which year you were born in). Why does the government care when you take the money? Because if it's in a pre-tax account, you've never paid taxes on ANY of the money yet . . . and the government wants its share! They don't want you to be able to keep growing the funds indefinitely without paying taxes.

Roth accounts do not have RMDs because the government doesn't care when you take out money that you're not paying taxes on anyway. And that means a lot more flexibility for you.

After all, if you reach your RMD age and you don't need the funds, why would you want to take a forced distribution? You'd rather let the funds continue growing tax-free for as long as possible—especially if the market is down and you'd otherwise have to take funds out of a declining asset! Roth accounts give you this flexibility to decide, entirely on your own, how you want to use your retirement assets.

They're also more tax-efficient and flexible if you pass away and distribute the retirement funds to your children. If you inherit any type of retirement account from a parent, you are going to have to distribute those funds over a ten-year period. (The 10-year rule is relatively new, by the way, as the beneficiary used to be able to spread out the IRA distributions over their life expectancy—which was great, as it allowed them to continue to benefit from the tax deferral for decades. Not anymore!)

The 10-year rule applies the same way whether you save money in a traditional IRA (pre-tax) or a Roth IRA.

(There's a lot more nuance to the 10-year rule in general, but if I write about it anymore, I will fall asleep at my desk—so I can only imagine how you're doing! Hang in there, we're almost done with this part!)

But here's where the situation differs in practice: Because you have to pay taxes on those pre-tax distributions, whenever they occur, your kids might be stuck with a huge tax bill during the ten-year period they're taking the funds out after inheriting the account . . . and if they're in their twenties or thirties, they may not have the resources to pay those taxes out of separate accounts (this happened to a client of ours who inherited her dad's 401[k] when she was twenty-seven!). Of course, inheriting money at all is a gift of love, but an inherited account that comes with a tax bill can be difficult to deal with.

The last point I'll make about the efficacy of Roth accounts is something we mentioned during the disability insurance section: I would rather pay the taxes when I'm healthy, working, and continuously earning more money, and not when I'm retired, not working, and on a fixed budget (even if it's a large amount!). This is the least technical reason to use Roth accounts, and arguably the most important!

This has all been a long way of saying that our chosen tax structure makes a huge difference in the long run. I know I came on strong here, but this is not to say that we only, and always, want to use Roth retirement accounts at the expense of saving into pre-tax accounts . . . it's not that black and white. In the interest of helping to paint a balanced picture, here are a few scenarios where you might prefer pre-tax retirement accounts:

- If you are on the cusp of a lower tax bracket in the current tax year, it might make sense to feed more money into your pre-tax retirement account to allow the deduction that comes with that contribution to push you into that lower bracket. (This is particularly important if we can go from the 32% to the 24% bracket in any given year.)

- You don't have any pre-tax retirement accounts. The standard deduction (or itemized, if that is more advantageous for you) means that the first $12,500 of ordinary income ($24,500 if married) is tax-free, regardless of the source. We want to make sure you have at least this amount generated for you in retirement from your pre-tax accounts, as doing so ensures that this pot of money is never actually taxed. Follow the thread: You didn't pay taxes on the traditional IRA contribution—it grew tax-deferred—and now, upon distribution, it fits under the standard-deduction 0% tax rate.

- You think you will be in a substantially lower tax bracket in retirement. Naturally, if you're in a higher tax bracket now than you think you will be in retirement, it would behoove you to defer the tax payment until the moment when your tax rate drops. (We alluded to this possibility earlier: While theoretically possible, I think this is one of the biggest misconceptions out there. If you are going to earn $400K+ for the balance of your working years, it's highly unlikely that in retirement you will be comfortable distributing only $50K annually. You will always have $100K to $200K in income coming to you, whether from part-time work, consulting, distributions from retirement accounts, real estate, capital gains, or other sources. Simply put, and from experience, your tax bracket will not be quite as low as you might think it will be in your retirement years, because people don't typically adjust their lifestyle on a dime [nor should they!]. What's more likely is that once you've hit a certain level of income/assets/lifestyle, you will be in the 24% tax bracket for the rest of your life, just by waking up in the morning.)

And this is to say nothing of the fact that tax rates across the board will (most likely) continue going up over the next twenty-plus years. For a more complete breakdown of why this is our approaching national reality, as well as to glean more detail on tax-efficient planning, please see the recording of my webinar at https://webinar.druckerwealth.com/.

I've tried to be balanced in spelling out the above, but my personal perspective remains that, while there are some reasons to build pre-tax retirement accounts over their Roth counterparts, they are all specific and, even then, should be done to a limited extent.

The reality is that for HENRYs, Roth retirement accounts are a huge opportunity. (I emphasize young people here because the longer time frame they have for their money to grow tax-free before they access it allows the Roth strategy to become more valuable.)

So how do we get more money into Roth accounts? It's a relevant question because 99% of our clients make too much money to contribute to a Roth IRA directly (their income being above the IRS threshold to do so). Instead, we can look to build Roth accounts through:

- Backdoor Roth contributions
- Mega backdoor Roth contributions
- Roth IRA conversions

A backdoor Roth IRA is a strategy by which you first add money to a traditional IRA with after-tax dollars (so you don't take any deduction like you normally would when you contribute to a pre-tax IRA). Then you convert the funds (i.e., move them) into the Roth IRA. Once the funds are in the Roth IRA, you can invest them however you'd like and take advantage of the normal benefits of a Roth IRA. The "backdoor" is just the term for the process by which you get the funds into the Roth IRA; it's not a separate account type. (Meaning, you wouldn't say you have a Roth

IRA and a backdoor Roth IRA. You only have a Roth IRA; you just might have used the backdoor Roth strategy to get the funds contributed.)

If that all sounds a little ridiculous and made up, well, it feels that way every time I explain it to a client, and every time we complete the strategy for our clients.

But it is an IRS-recognized strategy that most tax-focused planners will utilize if appropriate. While the point of this section isn't to force you to read the tax textbook from the CFP® exam, I'll just point out that you can't do a backdoor Roth IRA if you have pre-tax IRA money elsewhere in your plan. The IRS looks at all traditional IRA balances as one account, so if you were to convert only the after-tax account balance while you also have pre-tax IRA money, the IRS would look at this as a partial conversion of your total traditional IRA. We like to call this the "cream in the coffee" rule because IRA balances work like coffee: Once the coffee and the milk mix, you can't separate them out again. Same thing with pre-tax and after-tax traditional IRA contributions! I'm flagging this for you simply as a reminder & suggestion to do this sort of planning with a qualified tax professional.

The mega-backdoor Roth IRA (yes, this is a real name for a recognized tax strategy, though I'll understand if you find it hard to believe me!) is a similar maneuver, except it's done inside of your employer-sponsored 401(k). You can only do this *if* your company offers an after-tax 401(k) on top of the pre-tax and Roth 401(k)s, as this is a separate (and additional) account to make 401(k) contributions into. Most of the big tech firms (Meta, Amazon, Google, Apple, etc.) offer this after-tax 401(k), though you can confirm by reading through your 401(k) Plan Summary Guide (we look through this document for every new client, as it has a lot of helpful information about your 401[k] options!).

The backdoor contribution strategy is beneficial to utilize if you don't have a pre-tax traditional IRA balance, while a Roth conversion (which we're about to get into) is how you can get funds into a Roth even if you do!

A Roth conversion is when we convert your traditional IRA (which you may have because of a 401[k] rollover from a previous job or contributions you made when your income was lower) into a Roth IRA. Let's look at an example: You have $200K in your IRA, and we determine together that it makes sense to convert this money into a Roth IRA. This means, logistically, we are adding that $200K to your taxable income for the year. (So, yes, if you are in the 25% tax bracket, that $200K conversion will result in paying an additional $50K in taxes, which we will just assume you are paying out of your bank account.)

I know what you're thinking, *Whoa, that's a big tax bill!* Why did we do that? Well, now we have $200K sitting in a Roth IRA . . . forever! This means that in twenty years from now—when this account grows to $800K (assuming a 7% rate of return)—you will be able to distribute the full $800K tax-free. You chose to pay $50K today instead of paying $200K in taxes when you take the money out upon distribution (estimating a 25% tax bracket in the future as well). (This is a good time to remind you of what we talked about in Chapter 25: Effective tax planning is not about lowering your taxes in any given year but about using time to lower your lifetime tax liability. This also explains how tax prep/filing and tax planning are two totally different areas of focus.)

When are the most appropriate times to convert a traditional IRA into a Roth?

When you will be paying the least amount in taxes to do so! This is why market timing Roth conversions, like we alluded to at the start of the chapter, can be effective. Let's stick with the same example from earlier to explain.

We are looking to convert a $200K traditional IRA. But because the market is off 25% year to date, that $200K IRA is worth $150K right now. So, if we were to convert your traditional IRA right now, at its current low market value, you would be adding $150K to your taxable income this year instead of $200K (so you would save $13,500 in taxes by moving over the exact same number of shares in the portfolio)!

And even better . . . when the market rebounds, you are now benefiting from the market rebound inside of a tax-free account instead of a tax-deferred account, which means that the growth of that money just became intrinsically more valuable to you long term! Every dollar of growth in an account that is tax-free is worth a full dollar to you. Every dollar of growth in an account where you will eventually owe 30% to Uncle Sam means that you are only ever earning just 70% of that dollar.

Which account would you prefer to have your money in when the stock market rebounds?

28

Making Your Charitable Giving Count

"If not me, then who?"
– 1st Lt. Travis Manion,
who gave the ultimate sacrifice on April 29, 2007, on his
second deployment to Iraq. Travis won the Silver Star and
Bronze Star with Valor for his actions under attack, which
allowed every other member of his patrol to survive.*

* Please find the information about The Travis Manion Foundation
at the end of the book.

Every day, I pinch myself that I get to do my job. Partly, that's because I love talking to clients about money, investing, and tax strategy, and I can "nerd out" with anyone. But another huge part of it is that I get to help my clients realize their deepest convictions and help others. The high earners we work with at Drucker Wealth are some of the most amazing people I've met, and for many of them, a big motivator behind their hard work is giving money away, whether to charity or to their loved ones, and whether they've already started or they're setting it as a target for down the road. I love that I get to guide these conversations around giving.

In this chapter, we'll look at various options for sharing your wealth with the people and causes that are close to your heart—and how to make it work best for you, too.

Since many of our clients like being philanthropic (especially as they get older and feel more confident in their own financial trajectory), we spend time each year making sure they're making the MOST of their charitable giving when it comes to tax planning.

It's an area of planning that I'm passionate about, because supporting the meaningful organizations in my life is a huge part of my own financial plan. To that end, 100% of the proceeds from this book will go to causes and people near and dear to my heart. (Turn to page 367 for more information!)

As we dive into charitable giving, the first thing I always mention as a starting point—and I know this sounds obvious—is that you have to want to give money to charity . . . because you want to give money to charity! Your primary motivation for donating the money needs to be because you care about the cause and organization that you are supporting, not because of the tax benefit it provides you. I say this not as a moral critique (I'm not telling anyone they need to give to charity), but because of math! You will never come out "on top" giving away $1 and getting back $0.30 in tax savings . . . you are still giving away money!

Of course, assuming you WANT to give money to charity, there are ways of making your charitable giving count more under the tax code. I like to call it "lumpy" charitable giving.

Let's say you want to give $10K to charity each year and that even before you donate, you have $22,700 itemized expenses (from, for instance, mortgage interest taxes or state taxes). We'll assume, for this example, that you're married and filing jointly, which means your standard deduction would come out to $32,200. (To explain the tax situation briefly: Taxpayers can choose to take either the standard deduction or their itemized deductions, whichever is higher. Then, when calculating their taxes, this amount is excluded from their taxable income.)

Prior to you donating money this year, you would have taken the standard deduction (because you'd rather deduct $32,200 than $22,700), making your first $32,200 of your income tax-deductible—cool! If, however, you do make this $10K gift to charity, your itemized deductions would increase to $32,700. This would be higher than the standard deduction, so you would claim this higher amount on your taxes . . . an even better deal!

Except this strategy would mean that only $500 of that charitable deduction is truly deductible, because you were already benefiting from the $32,200 standard deduction in the first place! Put another way, if you had not donated anything, you would have benefited from the first $32,200 of deductions anyway, simply by taking the standard deduction. Your $10K charitable gift only resulted in $500 of additional tax deductions (and even less in actual tax savings), while $9,500 was eaten up by the standard deduction.

Let's say we mapped this out more efficiently and decided, instead, to make a $20K deduction every other year. With this, you're giving the same amount of money to charity over time, just at a different cadence.

In this scenario, in year one, you would have had $42,700 of itemized deductions (the $22,700 you already had + $20K in charitable giving). This means that you can now deduct $42,700 instead of the $32,200 resulting from the standard deduction. That's an extra $10,500 of tax deductions! So, working backward, that means $10,500 of your $20K charitable gift is essentially tax-deductible.

Again, in the first scenario, if you donated $10K evenly over the two years, only $1K total would have been tax-deductible ($500 each year). So that's $9,500 of addi-tional tax deductions just because you got "lumpy" with your charitable giving!

This is just one example. We could also take your giving a step further by setting up a DAF (Donor Advised Fund)—so that's what we'll talk about next.

Donor Advised Funds

Donor Advised Funds (DAFs) have become very popular over the last few years, and for good reason. A Donor Advised Fund is a type of account in which you deposit funds for the explicit purpose of making a full donation to charity over time.

When you contribute money to a DAF, you get a tax deduction in the current year for the full contribution, even if you wait a few years to disperse the money from the fund to the specific charities of your choice.

You get the full deduction up front because once you contribute the funds to the DAF, it is no longer your money. You have made an irrevocable gift to the fund, and it can only be used toward IRS-approved charities.

As an example: Say you want to donate $50K this year, but you're unsure which charities you want to donate to or when exactly you want to donate the money. You can contribute the full $50K to your DAF, receive the $50K tax deduction for the tax year, and then decide over the next few years how much you want to give, to whom, and when. The funds inside a DAF will grow tax-free until you are ready to disburse them. You get the tax benefit of the charitable donation all happening in the same tax year, but you still can feel like you're "giving" to the charity each and every year as you move funds out of your DAF.

Sometimes, it can make sense to put highly appreciated stock into a DAF, because you get the tax deduction for the current value of your donation, and you won't pay capital gains on the appreciated stock that you've moved over. If you want to donate $100K and you have stock that's worth $100K, but you only paid $20K for it, you may decide to offload the $100K into the DAF. The charity will receive the full $100K you wanted to give away, you will get the deduction for the full $100K of value that you contributed, and you don't have to worry about ever having to pay the capital gains on the stock. (Of course, it may be a really great holding that you want to keep, but that's a separate investment conversation.)

Whether you set up a DAF or not, gifting appreciated stock is a way of providing a meaningful sum to charity while removing a tax burden from your own situation: The charity doesn't have to pay taxes, and now you don't have to worry about that stock you bought twenty years ago, never sold, and don't know what to do with.

Again, win-win!

Before closing this chapter, I want to discuss what happens when you receive money from family members, and in particular, I want to reframe how your family might think about inheritance money.

This comes up quite often, and in my experience, there's some confusion as to how gifting and receiving monetary gifts works, in part because the taxes work differently than you would think they do.

Let's say your parents are giving you money for your kids—their grandchildren. If you're the recipient of a gift like this, there is nothing you need to do: no filing and no taxes to be paid upon receiving the money.

This is because it's the person making the gift who must be aware of the tax ramifications, not the recipient. In 2026, your parents (or anyone) can give $19K per person ($38K for a married couple) per beneficiary without having to file a gift return, and without any tax considerations. If they were to give any individual beneficiary more than $19K, they would need to file an additional tax form (Form 709) to let the IRS know what they were doing, but it wouldn't mean they owed any additional taxes that year. It would simply mean that the amount of the contribution that exceeded $19K would be documented and, ultimately, subtracted from their lifetime gift and estate tax exemption amount. For example: If you decide to gift $119K to family this year, you will have to file the additional tax form, and the excess $100K will be reported, lowering your lifetime gift/estate exemption from $13,990,000 to $13,890,000.

As of 2026, the current estate tax exemption is $15M ($30M if married and filing jointly), so it's not relevant to anyone but the highest net worth families—though this can always change, and it's something you absolutely want to monitor as you save and build wealth over time.

One last thing to mention while we're talking about inheritance . . . This is something I've thought about a lot after years of closely working with clients and hearing them discuss the finances of their already-retired parents. These clients often mention that they're going to get an inheritance one day—though, hopefully, not for two decades or more!

Here's what I've come to strongly believe: EVERYONE involved in this situation—the parents leaving the inheritance, their children in their early forties, and the grandkids who have no idea about any of this—would be happier and better off if the grandparents handed down this money to their adult children now! If the grandparents have done a great enough job planning and saving such that they're comfortably retired and will leave an inheritance, why wait until they pass away? Their adult children (in their forties) are in the busiest, most expensive phase of life (this is typically when folks are dealing with childcare, daycare, new housing costs, etc.) and that money will make the largest and most meaningful impact now, when things are (relatively) tight. That money is going to be a lot less impactful if the adult children end up inheriting it in their fifties or sixties. And if you're the grandparent and you know you're already going to give it away, don't you want your gift to be as beneficial as possible? Plus, this way, you'll be around to see the impact of your money. Maybe it will end up paying for summer camp, private school, or awesome family vacations—and you will get the endless joy of seeing that all happen in real time.

Of course, it's the grandparents' money: They don't need to give any of it away, nor should the kids feel entitled to a dime! But, if it IS important to the grandparents to leave money to their family, as it usually is, then coming up with a strategy for gifting NOW rather than waiting might be in the best interest of the entire family!

So we've covered how you can share your wealth with people and causes you care about. But what about one of the other things you probably care about most—educational opportunities for your kids and (someday) grandkids? That's where we're going next.

29

Saving Money for Your Children's Future

"Give your kids enough money so they can do anything, but not so much they could do nothing."
–Warren Buffett

Y̶ou'll be unsurprised to hear that when we work with new parents, they can't wait to start saving for their children's future! (Sometimes they reach out about opening a college savings plan when they're only a few months pregnant, and we tell them that while we love the energy, we have to wait until we have a name and Social Security number!)

There are several types of accounts you can utilize when saving for your children's future. While there is no one right or wrong answer, the type of account you choose can make a big difference! In this section, I will outline a few account types and options that should provide some context as you work through the various ways to allocate savings for your children's future.

Before diving into which account to start saving in, start by asking yourself:

- Do you plan to send your children to public or private school?
- Do you want to save specifically for college?
- Do you want to save more broadly for their future so you/they can use that money for life as it happens when they get older?
- Are there individual/personal events you want to start saving for? (Bar Mitzvah, sweet sixteen, sleepaway camp, first car, international trip, wedding, etc.)

Some of these might feel ridiculous to contemplate as you look over at your toddler (while the rest of you might be sweating as you think about your fifteen-year-old leaving the house in three short years), but it's just a way of thinking through what's coming around the bend!

More to the point, if you *know* that your daughter will have a Bat Mitzvah when she turns twelve, and you can see an account in your dashboard labeled "Rachel's Bat Mitzvah fund," you're going to be super motivated to save and grow that account over the next eight years!

529 Education Plans

A 529 education plan offers families a tax-advantaged way to save for education. Most of us know this. But I find that most people aren't aware of the flexibility and estate planning support that effective 529 planning can provide.

Let's start with the basics.

Money that goes into a 529 plan grows on a tax-advantaged basis and will be distributed tax-free if used for qualifying educational purposes (e.g., room and board, tuition, books, supplies, required fees, and computer-related expenses).

The 529 plans are not federally tax-deductible, so you do not save any money on your federal tax return by contributing to a 529 plan. But—and here's the piece that's relevant—most states do offer a state income tax deduction for contributions to 529 plans up to a certain contribution amount.

Every state has its own rules, and in some states, the deduction only applies if you use the state's specific plan. Let's run through a few state-specific examples as an overview:

- **Alaska, Florida, Nevada, New Hampshire, South Dakota, Tennessee, Texas, Washington, Wyoming:** None of these states have state income taxes (congrats to all of you living in these states!), so naturally, there is no deduction for 529 contributions. You can't deduct a tax you're not paying.

- **California:** Uniquely among the states, California doesn't offer ANY state tax deduction for contributing to 529 plans. A good rule of thumb when it comes to tax/estate planning is to assume that all California policy will lead to you owing the MOST amount of taxes possible for any given situation. I'm only 20% joking.

- **Massachusetts:** Only $1K ($2K if married filing jointly) of plan contributions are deductible on your Massachusetts tax return.

- **Minnesota:** Only $1.5K ($3K if married filing jointly) of plan contributions are deductible on your Minnesota tax return.

- **New York:** Up to $5K ($10K if married filing jointly) of plan contributions are deductible on your New York tax return.

- **New Jersey:** Up to $10K ($20K if married filing jointly) of plan contributions are deductible on your New Jersey tax return, but ONLY if you're below a certain income threshold. (For context, hardly any of our NJ clients are able to make a tax-deductible 529 contribution.)

- **Pennsylvania:** Up to $17K ($34K if married filing jointly) of plan contributions are deductible on your Pennsylvania tax return (so your full annual gifting amount).

The state tax deduction is a nice bonus, but the real reason people save into a 529 plan (and yes, I'm repeating this for emphasis) is that the money grows tax-deferred for as long as it stays in the account and then gets distributed tax-free if used for qualified education expenses.

So, what is considered a "qualified expense"?

- College tuition and fees
- Up to $10K for K-12 tuition, books, computers
- Up to $10K in student loan payments
- Special needs expenses for students who require them

You can also use 529 plans for education prior to college (in my experience, this is something most people aren't familiar with or aware of). Starting in 2026, up to $20K from your 529 account can be used toward K-12 education, trade schools, and student loan debt (it was only $10K in 2025). This is a great option since daycare and preschool costs these days feel almost as expensive as a college education. Or, for parents considering private school, you can now set aside money specifically for that purpose.

Sidenote: While this might sound like a smart strategy, the big advantage of having money in a 529 plan is tax-free growth for as long as the money stays in the account. So, if the account hasn't had time to grow (because you're using it to pay for sixth grade instead of waiting seven more years for college), you may not yield as much of the tax/ growth benefits as desired. Whether to use a 529 plan for these pre-college purposes ultimately will depend on your individual circumstances, but knowing that it's an option should be comforting.

Another unique feature of the 529 plan is the ability to pre-fund five years' worth of gifting. This is especially important for those with considerable assets. Family members can add five years' worth of contributions at once without running afoul of any gift tax rules. As the annual gift limit is $19K per year, this means you can contribute $95K ($190K if you're married) of contributions to the 529 in the first year and it's like you added $19K each year. The benefit of pre-funding the account like this is that it can lead to a few extra years of compounded tax-free growth.

These are the basics of a 529 plan. Now let's get into the lesser-known (and more interesting) use cases of 529 plans:

- You can change the beneficiary of a 529 plan to another family member at your discretion. So, the 529 plan may be meant for your daughter Amanda, but let's say she ends up getting a soccer scholarship that covers 100% of tuition. You can change the beneficiary on Amanda's 529 plan to your son Jack (who is set to go to school in three years) without any tax/penalty impact.

This also means that 529 plans can be passed down generationally and be an effective way to support your estate planning goals. For example, when my sister, Gabby, and I were born (twenty-two months apart), my dad set up a 529 plan for each of us and contributed to both plans each year. My parents ended up not needing to use the 529 plans when Gabby and I went to school, and as a result, the 529 plans continued growing tax-deferred during our college years. Here's the cool part. A few years back, my sister and her husband had a baby boy, so my dad transferred ownership of the 529 plan to them. He made my sister the owner of the account (rather than himself) and his grandson (my sister's baby boy)—the beneficiary. My sister gets eighteen-plus more years of growth, my dad moved an asset that is now both income-tax-free and gift-tax-free to his growing family, and that 529 plan can continue to serve as a flexible savings plan for any number of future Drucker grandchildren. (And yes, my dad let me know that I'd better have kids soon, or my sister gets the other 529 plan as well!)

- You can now also transfer a portion of your 529 balance into your own Roth IRA once you no longer are funding anyone's education. This new rule, which was only introduced a few years ago, helps you avoid feeling like you might overfund your child's 529. Let's say you have unused funds left over in your son's 529 plan and you have no more need for more education funds—you can now transfer up to $36K of the remaining balance into your Roth IRA without any penalties, taxes, surrender, or anything else! I suspect that this $36K 529-to-Roth limit will be expanded in the future, as the whole point of this allowance is to help people feel more confident using 529 plans (so fewer people need to take out student loans) without feeling like they're backing themselves into a corner.

That being said, the extent to which people feel like they're backing themselves into a corner by overfunding 529 plans mostly comes down to a lack of awareness about their options, as there really are no truly bad outcomes after you've put money into a 529 plan. In the absolute worst-case scenario, where you need to take non-qualified distributions (i.e., distributions not for education) from a 529 plan, you will pay a 10% penalty on the earnings and ordinary income taxes. A 10% penalty may sound like a lot, but remember, this penalty only applies to the earnings you've made in the account, not to the contributions.

So, if you've put $50K into your 529 plan over the last ten years, and it's currently worth $70K, then the 10% penalty only applies to the $20K of growth, meaning your total penalty, if you were to withdraw the full balance, is $2K. Manageable. And the income taxes are even less of a concern. You would be paying those taxes upon distribution if you contributed that money to a 401(k) anyway. When you consider that college costs are rising faster than inflation and that 529 plans are more flexible than they've ever been, the worry about overfunding them or not having options if your children go in a different direction is dramatically overstated!

UTMA/UGMA

First, what are UTMA/UGMA accounts and what do they actually do?

UTMA stands for Uniform Transfers to Minors Act, while UGMA means Uniform Gifts to Minors Act. They are both types of custodial accounts used as a means for transferring property to a minor.

You can set one up at any financial institution, just like opening a savings account, but there are some very important rules governing the UTMA/UGMA that you'll want to pay particular attention to.

Key facts about UTMA/UGMA accounts:

1. **Money placed in UTMA/UGMA accounts is an irrevocable gift.** This means the money can't be taken back and must be invested and used exclusively for the benefit of the minor.

2. **The beneficiary becomes the owner at the time of the gift.** Since this occurs while they are still a child, someone has to manage or oversee the funds.

3. **The person overseeing the funds is known as the custodian of the account.** This is usually the parent, grandparent, or guardian.

4. **Once the child reaches the age of majority—either eighteen or twenty-one, depending on the state you live in—the custodian is required to give the funds over to the child, and the money becomes theirs to use in any manner they wish.** If you are the beneficiary of a custodial account, make sure you are familiar with these rules because your financial institution (or parent) may not proactively reach out and give you the money on your eighteenth (or twenty-first) birthday. You'll likely need to contact them and request that it be transferred into your own account.

Funding a custodial account is easy, and there is no limit to how much you can put into UTMA/UGMA accounts. Since it is a gift, those gift tax rules we talked about in the last section kick in if you exceed the annual limits.

Quick point: Be wary of transferring money from UTMA/UGMA accounts into a 529 college savings plan, as the money retains its irrevocable nature and will be placed in a special "Custodial 529." This means you lose the ability to change beneficiaries down the road, like you can do in a traditional 529.

The calling card of custodial accounts is that any income earned from these accounts is considered "unearned income" of the child, and the first $2,200 is taxed to them. Amounts over this limit, which could be from capital gains, interest, or dividends, are taxed to the parent.

If you want to set aside money for your child or grandchild that isn't earmarked for a specific purpose, the UTMA/UGMA custodial accounts may be for you. Unlike a 529 college savings plan, money in a custodial account does not have to be used for anything specific. Despite this flexibility, the account does come with a more draconian mandate for how you need to distribute funds at the age of maturity. When your child reaches the age of maturity (usually eighteen or twenty-one, though it depends on the type of custodial account and the state), you need to hand over the money, regardless of whether you think they're financially ready or mature enough to handle it!

Many parents want to set up accounts to be used for something important and specific, and the lack of parental control means you're giving up that intentionality to a degree. You might want the money to be used as a down payment on a first home, car, or engagement ring, but with the UTMA/UGMA, you can't really make that call. You can have the convo with your children, but if they decide to go against your wishes, pull the money out, and party in Cabo . . . well . . . they can. While I don't actually think too many parents are worried about this sort of reckless behavior, it highlights the overly complicated nature of custodial accounts more broadly.

While the point of this book isn't to provide personalized advice, I'll admit that I'm not the biggest fan of these sorts of custodial accounts. I don't think there's enough reason to give up control; they can be a hassle to transition or change the titling of when your child is of age, and all else being equal, I default to wanting to keep things simple!

One alternative to keep things simple and flexible is to open a joint brokerage account with your spouse and nickname it "Johnny and Sam's Account" (or whatever your kids' names are). You would then earmark this account in your financial plan (and in your head) as being for Johnny and Sam's future benefit. You still own the accounts and can use them for whatever you want, but organizationally, you know that money is set aside for your kids' future. I love this approach when paired with the 529 plans. Hopefully, this additional context gets your wheels turning a bit as you think about the most efficient ways to set your children up for success!

30

Health Savings Accounts: The Holy Grail of the Tax Code

*"If I knew I was going to live this long,
I'd have taken better care of myself."*
–Mickey Mantle

I love seeing clients fund a Health Savings Account (HSA) because HSAs are among the most tax-efficient vehicles in the tax code. In fact, they are the only ones I am aware of that are triple-tax-qualified (tax-deductible contributions, tax-free growth, and tax-free distributions).

We'll get there, but let's start with a review of the HSA basics.

First off, only employees covered by High Deductible Health Plans (HDHPs) are allowed to contribute to an HSA. Of course, there are pros and cons to the different health insurance plans your employer may offer. It's beyond the purview of this book or even your personal financial planner to tell you which plan makes the most sense for your family, as it depends on the doctors you visit, the medicine you take, and other personal health details—but all the same, we ALWAYS strive to provide context to clients to help them understand their options. (Yes, your financial planner should absolutely be going through your employee benefits and health insurance with you!)

For additional context, an HDHP plan with a Health Savings Account typically has the lowest monthly premium costs but (as the name suggests) a higher deductible before the insurance starts to kick in. It's about deciding which costs you're most comfortable with.

Personally, I have always opted for the HDHP plan because I'd rather have lower monthly premiums and access to an HSA, and because I'm okay paying a few thousand dollars extra out of pocket if I need to. This last point is crucial. Choosing the high-deductible plan might not work out for me in a year if something bad were to happen—I'd have higher costs than if I had elected a different plan. This is something to bear in mind as you choose your own plan.

Now, let's consider HSAs in more detail. I mentioned, like an excited schoolchild, that they are triple-tax-qualified. Here's what that means:

- HSA contributions consist of pre-tax dollars (or they're deductible for people who aren't using payroll deductions to fund their HSAs, which gets us to the same outcome).

- Any interest earned on the account is tax-free, and you can direct the balance of your accounts into whatever index funds and mutual funds are available inside your plan. This means you can benefit from market returns inside an account that doesn't generate any taxable income or capital gains.

- Withdrawals for qualified healthcare expenses are always tax-free.

- If you never have any health care costs ever again (cool!), you can withdraw the funds at age sixty-five without any penalty! (You will just pay ordinary income tax on withdrawals, which means the worst thing that can happen with an HSA after you're sixty-five is that it's treated like a 401[k]!)

Taken together, these four facts create a powerful long-term investment tool. And it would be for nought except this one central fact: This money doesn't have to be used in the current year, and the full amount automatically rolls over year to year like any other investment account you own. (In this way, it's different from a Flexible Spending Account [FSA], which is available even without a high-deductible health care plan and therefore is a bit more common.)

Now, let's discuss the way to optimize everything the HSA has to offer.

In my experience, even clients who understand the logic of an HSA and are contributing to these powerful vehicles are still missing out on valuable tax benefits by not steering their HSA balances toward long-term investments. By investing in our HSAs like our other long-term investment portfolios, we are building ANOTHER asset that's outpacing inflation and that one day you will be able to distribute tax-free. Given this, the best thing you can do with your HSA invested balance—all else being equal and assuming you don't need the funds—is to let it grow indefinitely and use other means (like bank accounts) to pay your doctor co-pays and deductibles as you need to.

Why?

Because the growth is all tax-free, a dollar of growth in an HSA is worth up to 30% more than a dollar of growth in a savings or brokerage investment account. Put another way, you want to avoid interrupting tax-free compounding, wherever it exists, whenever you can!

31

Permanent Life Insurance: Friend or Foe?

"You can't put a value on human life, but my wife's insurance company made a pretty fair offer."
—Anonymous

Permanent life insurance leads to some of the most contro-
versial and fraught conversations in the entire financial
planning space.

Most of the fault lies with aggressive insurance agents.
Too many insurance agents talk about permanent life insurance (Whole Life, IULs, etc.) like it's the best thing since
sliced bread, and use convoluted and nonsensical terms like
"infinite banking," "divorcing yourself from Wall Street,"
and "becoming your own bank" to confuse the consumer
into forgetting that they are buying life insurance! They find
a way to turn any financial planning conversation into an
argument for why you should own (and own a lot) of cash-
value life insurance. By the way—and we'll get into this in
the section about finding a fiduciary financial advisor—an
unfortunate number of these insurance agents call themselves financial advisors, yet don't have a securities/advisory
license, which means literally the only thing they are legally
allowed to sell and advise on is life insurance!

But while these agents should be ignored entirely, there
is a subset of financial planners who take the other extreme
position and seem to think there is never a good reason to
own permanent life insurance. While this is nowhere near
as damaging, I don't think this is quite right either.

Permanent insurance, like any financial instrument, is
neither good nor bad—it's just a tool. It is appropriate in
certain instances and wildly inappropriate in others. As

I've said earlier, I think any financial professional (I use the term "financial professional" because they are largely not financial planners) who acts like a financial instrument is either "all good" or "all bad" is trying to sell you something. I will start by saying that I absolutely do not think permanent insurance is necessary or appropriate for most people at most times for most of the reasons it's sold. But permanent insurance can be a great vehicle if used in specific and limited circumstances (and I own it myself). There is a time and a place for it . . . and that's what this chapter is about.

So, when does cash-value life insurance make sense? Simply put, when you want *lifetime* insurance coverage!

Having permanent insurance means that your beneficiaries will receive a tax-free lump sum of money, whether you die at forty-five or eighty-five. If it's important to you that your beneficiaries are left with a non-trivial amount of money, no matter how long you live, then permanent insurance is worth looking into!

Having permanent life insurance might also give you peace of mind that you can one day spend down your retirement assets as much as you want, and your beneficiaries will still have a guaranteed amount coming to them when you pass. If you are legacy-minded, this might be super important to you! But what's the key here? To remember you are buying permanent insurance because it is *life insurance*, and you *want the insurance coverage.*

I emphasize this because, too often, permanent life insurance is sold for reasons that have nothing to do with the actual death benefit being provided. If legacy planning is not important to you, then quite frankly . . . we should *not* be discussing permanent life insurance, regardless of what other names people have for it. I'd also add that, even if you are legacy-minded and interested in helping your kids on a guaranteed basis, I would still suggest that the immediate priority is to make sure you're setting *yourself* up for financial flexibility and independence.

This means:

- You are *maxing out* your retirement accounts.
- You are saving *at least* 25% of your gross income annually.
- You are *on the right track to retirement,* so you can afford to start thinking about legacy planning and estate maximizing.

In other words, I view permanent life insurance as a luxury that should be turned to only once you've satisfied all of your foundational needs, and only if legacy planning is important to you.

The second clear use case for permanent insurance is as an estate-planning tool for high-net-worth families.

Life insurance proceeds are both tax-free and estate-tax-free, and so exist outside of federal income and gift tax laws. As a result, permanent life insurance affords a high-net-worth family fantastic leverage. If you can pay $1 today (which, if you are a high-net-worth family, you don't need and are not spending) to create an additional $4 (tax-free) upon your death, why wouldn't you? You can earmark that money for your family, a trust, your favorite charity, or any other purpose, and you're benefiting from the leverage between the premium payments and the death benefit.

Here's a more specific example: Let's say your mom has $1M in an IRA/401(k) that she is never going to spend down, and which you and your siblings will one day inherit. Receiving a "beneficiary IRA," as explained earlier, means you will have to pay income tax on the proceeds (because it's a pre-tax account and was never taxed), and you will, most likely, need to distribute all the funds over ten years according to the inherited IRA distribution rules discussed earlier. Simply put, you are about to get crushed by taxes and unwanted distributions whenever you inherit that IRA. What a hassle!

Instead, let's say your mom buys a life insurance policy and pays for it with $200K she takes out of the IRA while she is alive. She now has a permanent policy with a $1.5M death benefit. Now, when your mom passes away, you (and your mom's charities or other family members if she's so inclined) will receive $1.5M tax-free and estate-tax-free, and you can distribute the funds however you'd like, whenever you'd like. Your mom just turned $200K that you would have paid 40% taxes on (minimum) into $1.5M *tax-free*. If she's not spending the money anyway, why not create more leverage?

279

32

Starting a Business and Paying Your Kids

"My father didn't tell me how to live; he lived and let me watch him do it."
–Clarence Budington Kelland

In this chapter, we're going to cover two ideas that seem disparate—but bear with me, there's a reason we're covering them together! There are two questions I hear from folks all the time, and I'm going to answer them both here because I want to provide some tough love, on behalf of tax planners around the country, to the people who need to hear it!

Starting a Business

The first question is, "Should I start a business to lower my taxes?"

Every time someone asks this, my immediate reaction is to feel that there must have been a part of the conversation I missed. My response is generally to ask, "Well, do you have a business that you think you can make money from, or if I say yes, are you going to start brainstorming business ideas?" Because you should only start a business if you have an idea, product, or service you want to sell and that you think you can generate revenue from. In short, you should start a business if you already should be starting a business outside of any tax consideration. The idea of making up a business just to start deducting your personal expenses is . . . just a bad one. You're only asking for trouble (and the tax code doesn't work like that).

Don't get me wrong; if you have self-employment income, there are some great tax advantages and specific tax strategies to utilize, like:

- Deducting expenses attributable to the business
- Deducting a home office if you work from home (or separately, if you don't, utilizing the Augusta Rule to rent your home to your business for under fourteen days)
- Increased access to tax-deferred retirement accounts, such as Solo 401(k)s, Solo Roth 401(k)s, or SEP IRAs
- Setting up an S Corp so you can pay yourself a W-2 salary and take profit distributions to lower self-employment tax
- Paying your spouse and kids for legitimate work (and then reinvesting your kids' money into a Roth IRA now that they have earned income)
- Potentially qualifying for the qualified business income deduction to lower your taxable earned income

But as we've become fond of saying, "Taxes are a passenger on the bus; they shouldn't be driving the bus."

In other words, we want to make sure you're planning for what makes the most sense for your entire financial situation, rather than trying to fit a round peg into a square hole purely to minimize taxes.

We want to make decisions that align with your goals, financial priorities, and lifestyle, and *then* make sure we are doing it tax-efficiently.

By the way, these conversations are eerily similar to my introductory calls with prospective clients who say they want to "get into real estate." When I start asking questions like: "Where do you want to buy your first property?", "Do you want to do short-term or long-term rentals?", "Will you hire a management company?", "What does your cash-on-cash return need to be for you to be comfortable?"—they usually brush my questions aside and say, "I have no idea . . . I just want to lower my taxes."

Paying Your Kids

The second question I hear often is, "I've heard that I can pay my kids . . . and even set up a Roth IRA for them. What do you think?"

We've probably all heard that paying your kids is a game-changer when you're a small business owner. It's true, and it can be an effective tool, so let's dive into how this works, when it's appropriate, and when it's not.

First off, this strategy is only available if you are self-employed or a business owner. You can't be a W-2 income earner and "pay" your kids.

To address the second part of the question, you can set up a Roth IRA for your children, regardless of how you're paid, but you can only do so if they have earned income to contribute to the account.

Assuming you do have self-employment income, why does paying your kids feel like a home run? Let's say you earn $345K per year (meaning this net business income is reported as 1099 income on your Schedule C), and you have two kids aged ten and eleven. You want to pay them each $13K per year for "cleaning/administrative tasks." The first tax benefit of this strategy is that the $26K you pay them is deducted from your income as a business expense/write-off. With that, your Schedule C income is only $319K—cool!

Next, this income/salary will show up on your kids' tax returns. But here's the crucial part: Because this amount of income fits under the standard deduction, it will all be taxed at the 0% tax rate. (The first $15,750 of your income—as a single taxpayer—gets eaten up by the standard deduction, and so any income under this amount isn't taxed.)

So, effectively, you're moving this income from your own tax return (which would be taxed at the 32% tax rate) to your kids' tax returns, which will, most likely, fall under the standard deduction amount and be taxed at a 0% rate. In this example, this strategy would mean approximately $8,320 in tax savings.

So that's why it works. Now, let's discuss some rules and ideas for making it work for *you*, because you need to be realistic and use common sense when implementing this strategy effectively.

- First off, you can't pay your kids $50K per year for "office cleaning" if you've never paid anyone else close to that amount for cleaning prior to hiring your kids. I mean, you can, but this will be a giant red flag to the IRS. You have to make sure you're paying your kids an appropriate salary for the work they're doing, and a good way to gauge that is by asking the following two questions: "What would I pay someone else to do similar work?" and "Is this a job or responsibility that normally exists in my business, or am I creating it to pay my kids?"

- The work that you're hiring your kids to do has to be age-appropriate and something they are capable of doing. An eleven-year-old is not going to handle your bookkeeping or put together presentations for clients. But maybe they can organize your files, clean the office, do administrative tasks, or post pre-approved content to social media. (These are some of the most common tasks we see kids performing for their parents' businesses.)

- There's an IRS case study where a seven-year-old was confirmed eligible to work in their parents' business; yes, the IRS said this was acceptable! So, this is thought of, broadly, as the minimum age for working. Again, this isn't a rule or law, but a lot of tax practitioners will use age seven as a "best practice" based on the case-study precedent. (You should also check the child labor laws in your state.)

- If your child is younger than this, the only thing you can realistically hire your kid to do is model for your website, marketing videos, storefront photos, and similar tasks. Again, I would suggest using common sense here. Does your business really "derive income" based on pictures of your kids? Do you have other "models" you also work with or have hired in the past? Is this a core part of your business? Are you using one picture of your kid on your website and paying them $13K for a single shot? The more you stretch things, the more risk you create for yourself, and I just don't think any of it is worth the potential liability or hassle from the IRS.

- All of this is almost beside the point because you should be hiring your kids to *do* the work, documenting their hours and responsibilities, and then figuring out their total pay after the fact. You should not be figuring out how much to pay them first and then trying to find the responsibilities and hours to make it fit.

- To that end, you don't want to pay your kids exactly the amount that they will land just under the standard deduction. You don't want to pay your kids $16,0000 per year as a way to get as close to the standard deduction as possible, without going over. That's another giant red flag—a clear sign you're only interested in the benefit, and that you might just be trying to squeeze a round peg into a square hole to get there.

- A quick note: If you have an S Corp (which means you should already have a payroll system), there will be a bit extra to navigate, because you would have to pay your kid out of the S Corp (which means paying Social Security and Medicare taxes, which together are called FICA taxes).

From my own perspective and experience working with clients, I believe the primary benefits of hiring your kids should be the experience they gain in learning a skill, the values and work ethic you can instill in them through hard work, and the sense of accomplishment from completing a task. If this is the starting point, it becomes a lot simpler and more comfortable to incorporate the tax benefits associated with the activities, because you will have the records, the hours log, and the details to put forth your case if you are ever questioned by the IRS.

For 95% of you, this section might have seemed irrelevant—and that's okay! For one thing, these ideas might have been somewhere in the back of your mind, even if it turns out you can't implement them yourself. But more importantly, the overall goal here is to become more intentional with your financial decision-making. Having a better sense of the strategies that you can utilize—and those you can't—will help you become clearer about the gaps in your own planning and where you might want to focus your energies.

33

Intro to Restricted Stock Units

"Room for error—often called margin of safety—is one of the most underappreciated forces in finance. It comes in many forms: A frugal budget, flexible thinking, and a loose timeline."
–Morgan Housel

If you're like the overwhelming majority of our clients, you've likely been granted Restricted Stock Units (RSUs) as part of your compensation package. Being on the receiving end of RSUs is a wonderful thing, especially if you are a mid-career professional with time to make the most of your vested shares as part of your broader financial plan.

The first part of this section might feel a bit basic, but bear with me! Even if you have been receiving RSUs for a long time and understand how they work, there's utility in understanding them compared to other types of compensation, stock options, and investments. It might help provide a new way to think about them.

To that end, let's begin with what RSUs are not:

- They are not stock options.
- You do not have to "exercise" your RSUs.
- You do not have to compare your strike price with the market price and then decide if it's the right time to pull the trigger (like you would with Incentive Stock Options, ISOs).

RSUs are simply your company's promise to compensate you with company stock if you satisfy certain conditions, which, by the way, is the exact same framing as your base salary, even if we don't think of it in the same way! Your salary is a promise to compensate you with cash if you satisfy certain conditions (i.e., if you do your job!).

What Conditions Are Often Tied to This Equity Compensation Incentive?

- **Vesting Schedule:** We often see a four-year vesting schedule with a one-year cliff. This setup means that 25% of your RSUs vest one year after they were granted, and the remaining 75% vest proportionately each month/quarter over the next three years. At the end of four years, assuming you're still at the company, you would have earned 100% of the shares specified in the original grant. At this point, provided you haven't sold the shares yet, you simply own the shares you've been granted, and they will sit in your brokerage account like any other stock that you bought on the open market.
- **Performance Benchmarks:** This is company/role-specific, but you can receive RSUs that vest upon the company, your team, or the stock price clearing certain performance hurdles.

What's the Best Way to Think About My RSUs?

It's simple: RSU grants are just another type of compensation! Perhaps you make $300K in base salary, $75K in bonuses, and have 100 RSUs vesting each year. Well, just like you don't have to "pay" anything to obtain this base salary, you don't have to "pay" anything to obtain these RSU shares when the time comes. They are simply deposited into your account when they vest.

The point I am making here is that RSUs are intrinsically valuable. There is no cost attached to your RSUs (i.e., you don't pay anything to receive the shares), so you're always "in the money" when you receive them. Just like your salary or bonus, there's almost never a situation where your RSUs aren't worth something. (This is unless the company goes out of business or the stock price falls to zero, which, while possible, is unlikely with the companies we most commonly see.) We always encourage our clients to check their specific plan rules and remember: the value of RSUs depends on the company's stock price at the time they vest.

The intrinsic value of RSUs is one of its key distinctions as compared to other types of equity compensation. For example, if you are given ISOs (Incentive Stock Options), you have the right to buy shares at a set price, which is *usually* a discounted price. But if you have the option to buy your company stock at $40 per share, and the current market price is $35 per share, your options are effectively worthless—you'd be better off just buying your company stock on the open market, just like anyone else. In that case, you would never choose to exercise that option, and all your ISOs would be hypothetical. If you don't exercise that option, you never actually get those shares! This is why RSUs are much more comparable to your base salary than stock options, even if they're not typically framed like that. It's true that, unlike your salary, you don't know the exact value of your RSUs until they vest (because the stock price changes every day), but it's still guaranteed compensation as long as you're employed.

How Are RSUs Taxed?

To illustrate the tax treatment of RSUs, let's say you earn $300K in base salary, $75K in bonus money, and 100 RSUs. When tax time comes around, your taxable income will be $375K plus the market value of your 100 RSUs on the day they each vested, because your vested RSUs just stack on top of your other W-2 income.

In other words, the tax treatment of your vested RSUs is identical to your regular compensation (W-2) income. This means you are responsible for paying ordinary income tax on the value of those shares on the day they vest.[28] Using the same example—if 100 RSUs vested this past Monday, and the price at that time was $325 per share, then you just added $32,500 to your taxable income for the year. (How I got there: $325 x 100 shares = $32,500.)

This is the key from a tax standpoint: What you choose to do with the stock after Monday's vest has nothing to do with this tax liability. You are responsible for paying taxes on that income, regardless of whether you choose to sell or hold onto the shares.

Alternatively, let's imagine that your company (instead) gave you a $32,500 cash bonus on Monday and you decided to take that $32,500 and buy company shares on the open market.

In terms of stock ownership and tax liability, the two situations are the exact same. In both scenarios, you will be taxed on $32,500 as ordinary income, and in both scenarios, you now own company shares and need to decide how long you want to hold them or when to sell.

If you were to sell your company shares on the same day they vest (or close enough to it), there would be negligible capital gains/losses, because the price wouldn't have fluctuated from the purchase price/vesting price, and you're already responsible for the expectant income tax liability based on the vesting price. Alternatively, if you choose to hold onto the stock indefinitely, you will be responsible for paying capital gains on the distribution whenever you do sell.

How Do Taxes Get Paid When RSUs Vest?

There are different ways to pay the income tax on RSUs when your shares vest. Most people elect "sell to cover" when choosing how they want their vested RSUs paid out. This means that if 500 shares vested this past Monday, you would receive 350 shares, and the company would hold back the other 150 shares to pay your tax liability up-front. (I'm making up the exact ratio here, but you get the idea.)

This is done to avoid being hit with a gigantic tax bill at tax time. If you chose not to withhold any shares for taxes, you would realize the following April that you owed the government *a lot* more money. (As a comparison, it would be like having no withholdings from your paychecks for three months straight!)

There's one additional point to note, as sometimes new clients come to us confused and frustrated that they still owe taxes even after selling some of their RSUs explicitly to cover their taxes (and understandably so!). Here's where the problem comes from: RSUs are typically withheld at the 22% federal tax rate. If you are in the 28%, 32%, or 37% tax bracket, and your RSUs are being taxed only at a 22% withholding rate, then there's going to be an underpayment of tax throughout the year that will leave you with an unwanted tax liability come tax time.

So, what can be done to avoid a surprise tax bill? It can be helpful to set up quarterly estimates with your tax preparer—something we do with the majority of clients whose taxes we prepare. Once your CPA understands your withholding rate, extra income via RSUs, filing status, retirement contributions, and so on, they will be able to figure out how much you might owe on top of your current payments and set up a program to pay that amount proactively throughout the year (e.g., paying the IRS an additional $3K per quarter so you don't owe anything come tax time).

As a good rule of thumb, if you consistently owe the IRS money come tax time, and especially if you have RSU grants, it probably means you should be setting up quarterly estimates to eliminate any unwanted surprises. For our clients, we strive to ensure that your tax planning and prep have the same level of intentionality and purpose as your financial and investment planning. (Of course, it's a lot easier for us to do this since we typically handle our clients' financial planning, investment, AND tax filing needs!)

34

Restricted Stock Units: Planning for Your Future

"There are only two kinds of money: wealth and money that runs out."
—Nick Murray

Hopefully, the last chapter wasn't all you could handle reading about your restricted stock units (RSUs), because we're about to go deeper. While the previous section was structured to help you understand how RSUs work, this next chapter is about understanding what to do with your stock once it's vested and you own it.

To that end, I'm always fascinated by how people think about their employer stock.

- Do they think it's their meal ticket to unbridled wealth?
- Do they view vesting RSUs as another source of liquidity with which to pay the bills?
- Do they think about it similarly to their 401(k)—that it's not really "money" until retirement?

There's no one "correct" answer, but there are helpful frameworks and ways of thinking through what to do with your RSUs that can lead to better outcomes over time. I've seen prospective clients do just about everything possible with vested company stock. I once had a prospective client at Google tell me during their Right Fit call that every time their RSUs vest and their trading window opens, they sell ALL of them immediately and then move that money to their savings account.

When I asked why, they said, "Not sure. I started doing it a few years back and kind of just got used to it . . ."

I've spoken with a young woman who has built up over $1M in Facebook stock over the years, to the point that this one company's stock makes up over 90% of her family's net worth . . . and she hasn't sold a dime! She told me she knows she probably should sell, but she hasn't been able to pull the trigger.

I could keep going, but I would say the common thread in most of the RSU stories I hear is that a lot of these decisions are made through inertia. The RSU holder hasn't put together a full financial plan—one that incorporates their company stock into the mix—so, not really knowing what to do, they take the path that seems easiest and most comfortable.

To avoid finding ourselves in this situation, what questions should we be asking ourselves when it comes to our vested stock, and when should we be selling it?

My starting point is always this: There are only two fundamental reasons to sell company stock that we've accumulated:

1. Cash flow
2. Diversification

We can put this another way. The two scenarios in which we might sell RSUs are: *Selling from a position of weakness/ need or from a position of strength/opportunity.*

Let's start with the first reason: cash flow. If you have a substantial amount of company stock (whether in the form of RSUs that have vested, ISOs that you exercised, or employee stock purchase plan contributions), but you also have some credit card debt hanging over your head or are lacking an emergency fund, then company stock can and should be thought of as a godsend.

Before we can focus as extensively as we want on the planning aspect—investing, retirement planning, and tax coordination—we need to make sure there are no creaks in the floorboards.

Eliminating credit card debt should be the very first priority in a financial plan, especially if you are a six-figure earner with other assets. Honestly, credit card debt should not even be something you're willing to stomach! (And when I say debt, I mean that you have had an outstanding balance for more than thirty days and it is actively accruing interest against you.) If you have $300K in vested company stock and $10K in credit card debt, selling to eliminate that debt should at least be seriously considered

Part of this is about habits and drawing a line in the sand: Credit card debt should not be part of our vocabulary at your income level. But part of this is just math. Credit card debt works against you to the tune of 19%, 20%, or even 29%. These are outrageous (and unacceptable) numbers! Maybe your company stock (or other investments) will reach those performance highs; it absolutely has happened in some years, but we don't know if it will again, whereas we *do* know that those negative interest rates will be there indefinitely until the debt is gone.

Moral of the story: If company stock allows you to do so, rip off the band-aid and consider your era of credit card debt over.

I would say something similar to someone who doesn't have their six-month emergency fund in cash. If you only have $10K in the bank but it costs you $50K to wake up each morning for the next six months, I'd want to see you take some of that equity and set up your lifetime emergency fund (this is NOT investment advice!). Having an adequate and comfortable cash cushion gives people the confidence to invest and stay the course, through good times and bad. They're never going to find themselves in a position of needing to sell their holdings in order to raise cash, pay taxes, pay for a trip, etc. It's a short-term sacrifice (moving the money to cash) to set up a foundation that will benefit you for life.

Those are the times when you want to look at selling stock because you "need to" rather than because you "want to." It comes from a position of fixing a problem rather than enhancing an opportunity.

Truthfully, this doesn't come up much for us, as most of our clients have all of this covered before they reach out to us. They have an emergency fund in place and have no outstanding credit card debt. And this actually makes the conversation around when to sell more interesting, because it becomes far more nuanced.

Simply put, if vested company stock makes up a disproportionate amount of your net worth, it might make sense to sell a portion of your company stock and then reinvest in a more diversified compilation of stocks to minimize your concentration risk. (I hesitate to give a specific percentage here because this is totally client-specific, but chances are, you will have a sense if this might apply to you.)

While we like to think your company will do well and grow forever, we don't know that for certain! Things happen. Any company can suffer through a rough period, lose 80% of its value in a few quick years, and never truly recover. Meanwhile, as you well know by this point in the book, this has never happened in the broader stock market.

Essentially, selling your concentrated position is like taking some chips off the table. Actually, it's more like cashing in your chips at the casino in return for hard-earned money that you know will pay for your next family vacation if you walk straight out the door. (By the way, I don't gamble, bet on sports, play the lottery, or do anything that can lose me money in two minutes based on things outside of my control, but the metaphor is too accurate not to use.)

Moving money from one company stock to a diversified portfolio means turning your hard-earned RSU income into being part-owner of thousands of companies that have, while competing and replacing each other in your portfolio, generated 10% returns on an annual basis. In other words, by diversifying, you're giving up the (historically tiny) chance of earning incredible returns for the historical certitude of earning above-average returns for decades to come.

But like all financial decisions, this is totally client-specific, and once you start thinking through individual circumstances, a different picture might emerge. There are times when it makes sense not to sell your company stock because of its growth potential, your financial position, and your risk capacity (which, as discussed earlier, means your specific ability to take on outsized risk based on your financial flexibility and time horizon).

Two stories come to mind here.

I've been working with a client family for five or six years. When they initially reached out, they had a substantial position (a few million dollars) in a growth stock that had recently skyrocketed in value. It was obviously a huge part of their financial picture. Then, shortly after we started to work together, one spouse's father passed away, and they inherited a few million dollars (spread across retirement accounts, insurance proceeds individual stocks, etc.).

Suddenly, her outsized position in the stock didn't feel quite as dramatic. Even before their inheritance, they were super confident in the company (which had already borne out in the few years they had held the stock before we started working together) and felt that it had a lot more room to grow. We began modeling different options to help them understand their real risk capacity, and the models showed that, between the capital appreciation they had already benefited from and the inheritance they had just received, they were in fantastic financial shape.

If the company didn't continue to outperform the stock market—heck, even if it drastically underperformed the market—they were still on track to achieve all their financial goals. They were saving enough to fund their two boys' college educations, they were way ahead of expectations in their own retirement planning, and they had already been diligently saving for a new home for a few years so that goal was fully funded once they found a place they loved.

They were under no illusions and knew that keeping their stock would be a risk. Yet they were in the perfect position to take on some additional risks with their stock position, because even if their stock lost value, their financial plan would still look solid. We still sold some of their stock every year—it's simply a good idea to take some of your hard-earned profits and "top off" your stock position (i.e., sell 10% of your total position each year and move it into your broader portfolio) when you receive new RSU grants each year. This gives you the best of both worlds: You are maintaining/growing your stock position through new vests and the existing shares' growth, while increasing your non-stock net worth through the shares you're selling.

This strategy has worked fantastically for them. Over the last five years, we've sold over $1M of her stock position—adding it to the "boring" diversified part of their portfolio which allowed them to sleep better at night—while the stock itself has continued its torrid pace. This means that even as she has successfully turned a highly volatile single stock into real wealth for her family, she still holds a significant position in her company stock that will allow her to benefit from continued growth.

According to any financial textbook and even to Drucker Wealth's general RSU approach, they still have far too much concentration in one stock. That's true. But because of a series of events specific to their financial program (such as disciplined saving/investing prior to the stock "hitting," receiving an inheritance, living below their means for the last ten years, etc.), they were in the perfect position to take this risk with company stock they were super optimistic about.

As always, personal finance is more personal than it is finance.

The next story is about a new client who was a bit younger and earlier in her financial trajectory. On our first planning call, she brought up some advice an advisor at another firm had once given her. They told her to sell her vested stock (approximately $60K worth) in Meta to "diversify" into other investment portfolios (managed by them, of course!). She must have seen my face because she paused and asked, "You don't agree?" I began to consider how we think about company equity as it relates to risk, diversification, and growth potential. Short version: In my opinion, this client was in an ideal position to take some long-term risks by continuing to hold company equity.

Why?

- Her age: Being in her mid-thirties, she had a super-long time horizon and did not need this money anytime soon.

- She was making a great salary and bonus.
- She had zero debt.
- She had already built an emergency cushion to adequately cover six months of living expenses.
- Most importantly, she had the ability to save 30%+ of her gross income, which meant that even if the amount of stock represented more than 15% of her net worth RIGHT NOW, as she saved/invested more each year, it would inevitably make up less and less of the growing total. It didn't matter what her concentration level was this second but what it was trending toward over the next decade. There was no need to divert company stock for that purpose—and end up with a big tax bill to boot!

In other words, in my opinion, she's exactly the type of person who can usually afford to take some long-term risk with company equity in a way that won't negatively affect her other financial goals. This had the potential to be a worthwhile risk for someone at the start of their journey. Selling it "just to sell" didn't sit right with me.

The recommendation wasn't "bad" by itself, but it appeared to have been made without accounting for this person's specific financial picture and future goals. Generally, I don't like any financial advice that seems to be made in a vacuum or defaults to cookie-cutter recommendations simply because it's easier to treat every situation the same rather than have real conversations about risk capacity, scenario planning, and the best-case and worst-case outcomes of each decision.

For our younger clients in their mid-to-late thirties, who are being highly compensated in company stock, it's just a fact that their company stock will be a higher percentage of their net worth for a while. A forty-year-old who has established themselves in the tech space, is already a director, and who will most likely continue to be granted new company stock in the future, doesn't need to sell prematurely to avoid some artificial concentrated stock limit. It will happen with time, as long as we have a strategy.

And so, there are times when we may tell clients it's okay to keep a relatively higher percentage of their investments in their vested stock.

It's important to note that in both situations above, the clients wanted to continue to hold their company stock. If they didn't (or were ambivalent), these would have been different conversations. We never recommend continuing to hold company stock if clients don't have a preference. As you well know by now, I think holding individual company stock instead of investing in the broader market is an unnecessary and unknowable risk. Only if a client feels strongly about it, and if circumstances permit (like in the situations above), am I comfortable advising a client that it's okay to hold it.

I'll add briefly that using custom indexing portfolios—a strategy I introduced in Chapter 26—is an effective way of incorporating company stock into a diversified portfolio.

We do it all the time. As an example: say you have $1.1M in Google stock and you've owned the stock for years (so it has a super low cost-basis if you were to sell). You might want to sell a big chunk of stock (understanding that it's a huge position in one company's stock) but you know that you'll pay a boatload in taxes if you do!

Well, we could move a portion of the position into your custom index portfolio instead. The position would be treated as a part of the portfolio, and so we wouldn't need to buy other positions with similar profile and risk characteristics. Simultaneously, we would set up a "capital gains budget," which would allow us to control how much of the stock we want to sell in the coming years and ensure we're never generating more in capital gains tax than our clients are comfortable with. (There is another tactical strategy around concentrated stock and custom index portfolios we implement using covered calls, but I think it'd take us too far from the main point of the chapter. I'm just flagging it so as to acknowledge its applicability here.)

As a final point, while we never want to prognosticate on a company's future performance, we must also be honest with ourselves about the company we hold stock in. Most of our clients work at companies whose stock has done incredibly well over the last five to ten years. While this doesn't tell us much about its fortunes over the next three decades, it is only fair to acknowledge that holding company stock in established behemoths like Google, Amazon, Facebook, or Apple is not the same as taking a chance on a company that IPO'd six months ago and might not exist three years from now.

PART 4
HIRING AN ADVISOR: PICKING THE RIGHT ONE FOR YOU

"If you think it's expensive to hire a professional to do the job, wait until you hire an amateur."
—Red Adair

WHAT IT'S WORTH

WHAT IT COSTS

THE VALUE OF REAL ADVICE

BEHAVIOR GAP

As we approach the end of this book, I hope you feel better prepared to think about your own financial world and how to apply some of these foundational concepts to your family's planning.

In the first three parts of this book, I've been working to provide you with a deeper understanding of:

1. What real financial planning is (and what it isn't)
2. The foundational financial concepts and how they translate to financial decision-making
3. The tactical tax, investment, and insurance strategies that matter (and those that don't)

Now, the question is: Can you implement all of this on your own?

Or perhaps the better question is: Should you?

For most of you—especially those with demanding careers, family responsibilities, and complex financial situations—having a guide on this journey can be invaluable. The right financial partner doesn't just save you time. They can help you avoid costly mistakes, spot opportunities you might miss, and keep you disciplined when emotions threaten to upend everything you've worked so hard for.

The keyword here is "right." Not all financial advisors are created equal. Some are glorified product salespeople masquerading as advisors. Others are investment managers with little interest in comprehensive planning. Some charge fees that aren't aligned with the value they provide, and some simply aren't the right fit for your needs.

In this final section, we'll explore how to navigate these tricky waters. We'll discuss who might not be a good fit for ongoing financial planning/investment management in the first place (and why that matters). We'll explore why the implementation of advice matters more than the advice itself when it comes to measuring the value of financial guidance. We'll debunk common misconceptions about advisor compensation and explain the real value a great planner provides.

Along the way, you'll discover why having multiple advisors might actually be worse than having none, how to think about advisor cost in your decision-making, and most importantly, how to distinguish between someone who merely manages investments and someone who truly provides comprehensive financial planning.

By the end of this section, you'll have a clear framework for finding the right advisor for your specific needs. And as you'll see, this isn't just a blanket "You should hire my firm." We are selective about who we take on as clients, and we know we aren't the right fit for everyone!

To that end, we're going to start by explaining why a financial planner who is clear about who they *don't* work with should make you more bullish that they might be the right partner for you!

35

A Great Question to Ask a Prospective Financial Advisor

"Many people take no care of their money
till they come nearly to the end of it, and
others do just the same with their time."
–Johann Wolfgang von Goethe

One of the first questions you should ask any wealth advisor you're thinking about hiring is, "Who is not your ideal client? Can you provide me with some examples of clients who don't fit your firm?"

In my opinion, you don't want to hire a firm that will work with anyone and everyone. Because if there aren't clients who they're willing to walk away from, it probably means they also don't have a client type or an area of focus that they are especially adept at serving. And don't you want to find a financial planning firm that spends all day building expertise and talking to clients who are dealing with the same sort of financial issues and nuances you yourself are encountering?

If you are a high-income earner in your mid-forties, you probably don't want to work with a firm that mostly serves retirees. If you have $2M of assets, you probably don't want to work with an advisor whose average client has $500K. If you are a federal employee, you probably don't want to work with an advisor who specializes in working with business owners. It's not that they can't do great work for you; it's just that their firm wasn't specifically designed to do great work for you. And that difference matters! In today's world of Zoom meetings and virtual firms (like ours!), where geography has been made irrelevant, it's no longer enough to settle for an advisory firm because they are down the block.

The second reason this question matters is that it protects you from hiring the sort of advisor who will take on anybody and everybody because they are simply desperate for new clients. If they don't have a niche (or at least a general target client) and they're willing to take on anyone who will pay them, this can hint at two potential issues: 1) their value proposition is so weak that they can't seem to build a sustainable firm of right-fit clients, or 2) they are simply interested in accumulating clients like baseball cards, without paying much attention to the client's experience, the quality of service, or the longevity of the relationship.

If asking this question helps you to sniff out either possibility, it's a question worth asking! To give you a sense of what a "wrong fit" list might look like, here's the official Drucker Wealth Bad Fit List:

1. FIRE Movement Subscribers

If you're unfamiliar, the FIRE (Financial Independence, Retire Early) Movement refers to those who want to retire as soon as humanly possible and are willing to do whatever it takes to get there. This might mean not taking any vacations, downsizing the family home to the bare minimum, not going out to eat, not paying for TV/Netflix/HBO . . . basically, living an austere lifestyle to save up enough money to retire ASAP. Now, I'm not judging—there's nothing inherently wrong with this approach—it's just one that I don't think is the right fit for my firm and the way we think about money.

At Drucker Wealth, as I've mentioned, we believe that financial planning should help you strike the right balance between your current lifestyle and your future goals; between your current wants and future needs. To us, effective planning means helping our clients to enjoy life and maximize their time now, while knowing that they're not sacrificing their future goals in the process. I find the FIRE Movement especially stressful because not only does it mean sacrificing your current lifestyle to retire, it also creates a rigid, fixed-cost retirement since you will inevitably have to live on a set amount of money for the rest of your life.

My inevitable question for someone going through life like this is, "When does the fun part happen? When do you get to live?" To us, retirement is not a goal in and of itself. It reflects what really matters: your quest for financial independence. I am 100% confident in saying that most of my clients are less focused on age-driven retirement than they are on attaining financial independence.

To repeat the definition I gave earlier: Financial independence means doing what you want, with whom you want, when you want, for as long as you want. For some, this means full retirement at age fifty. For others, it means transitioning to part-time income or doing some consulting work or nonprofit work that feeds their soul. For others still, it means reaching retirement age and realizing that they still love what they do, are fully engaged, and have very little stress or restraints doing it—so why not keep the party going!

We work with clients who are journeying through each of these life paths, and my team and I enjoy mapping out these winding paths together with our clients over time. Maybe it's because I so thoroughly love what I do and find the journey of building my business as rewarding as any destination I might reach, but I just can't wrap my head around being motivated, beyond anything else, to completely stop building, growing, and accumulating.

2. Rental Properties/Passive Income Driven

We've spent enough pages discussing real estate and passive income, so this shouldn't be too surprising. We don't need to run through my biases again. (And while I think they are a helpful and accurate framework, they are, of course, biases!)

I'll just say this: In my experience, most people who bring up real estate on a first call aren't looking for it to be just another solid investment, like their 401(k), Roth IRA, or ETF portfolio. Instead, they expect it to work like some sort of magic pill that will allow them to retire twenty years earlier than they imagined.

Again, this is just my experience, but people who reach out looking to generate "passive" income via rental properties are usually looking to circumvent the planning work and time usually required to achieve lasting wealth. I have yet to see a rental property zealot achieve the lofty goals that they sometimes ascribe to their rental properties. As a result, I don't understand this impulse, nor do I see it as a viable path toward true financial independence.

3. $20M+ Liquid Net Worth

I know, this one is crazy for a wealth manager to admit. After all, who wouldn't want to work with clients who have all this money for us to manage? And yet, here we are.

Quite simply, the ultra-high-net-worth space is just not what excites me about what I do. To me, at a certain point, that would feel like working in the margins and without stakes. Instead, I like getting my hands dirty. I love working with clients who are looking to achieve their version of financial independence in the next twenty to thirty years and just need a plan of attack to get there. My team specializes in helping you define and design this financial roadmap, and we relish the opportunity to guide you over time as you strive to make financial independence your reality.

Most of my clients are high-income earners in their thirties and forties with a liquid (i.e., not real estate) net worth between $1M and $20M. This is where I think a fiduciary financial planner can provide the most value to the families they've partnered with and the capital they've decided to steward. (The fact that most of my team is in the same age range as our clients is not an accident either.)

Again, just like the FIRE Movement, this is not to say that ultra-high-net-worth families don't need financial planning support or wouldn't benefit from professional guidance. Of course they would! But they would be best served by firms that are designed exclusively to work with them.

4. Price Shoppers

Looking at a few different financial planners before deciding is normal, of course! I'm not saying you shouldn't do that—though I do think there's a point of overkill and that the right fit is the right fit, no matter how many other firms you look at. But alas!

When I talk about "price shoppers," I'm really referring to folks who decide on a planner based purely on who is the least expensive in the short term. Quite frankly, someone with this mindset is just not someone who thinks about planning in the same way Drucker Wealth does. Someone more focused on the short-term cost of our guidance than on the long-term value our services are designed to provide over the next twenty to thirty years, in both tangible dollars and financial clarity, probably isn't the right fit.

There's an old joke among business owners that a $500 per year client might have seventeen questions about contract stipulations, might change their mind five times, and might ask for a discount or more time to think about it, while a $50K per year client gets the invoice and just asks, "Is a check okay?" before signing or paying immediately.

The first time I saw this joke, it had nothing to do with wealth management, but I can confirm that it's spot-on for my industry (though I made up the exact numbers).

That $500 per year client is fighting against their nature, as they clearly don't want to pay for professional advice! If they really knew and believed in the value of advice, they wouldn't have any questions—except maybe to ask what the catch is, since the fee is so low!

We want clients who value professional expertise.

Of course, we want clients to do their homework and confirm our fees are reasonable—but we also want them to realize that paying the fee is the solution to getting what they need.

5. Jerks and People Who Just Want "Yes" Men and Women

This should really be first. My firm has a "no a**holes" policy when agreeing to take on new clients. We only work with reasonable and considerate people who appreciate the value of our services.

A financial planner's value to their client is only as good as the personal relationship allows it to be. We're some of the first people you tell about becoming pregnant or if you suffer a death in the family. We're there for job promotions and corporate downsizing. Sometimes our job is to provide tough love, and other times, it's to give you our encouragement to make a lifestyle change because your plan supports it. This doesn't always mean you'll agree with what we say or choose to do everything we recommend over time, but it does mean that every interaction is based on mutual respect and trust. We are committed to living our lives from a place of joy and kindness, and to building long-lasting, healthy relationships with each of our clients.

This is the only type of long-term relationship we know how to build. It's the only one that allows you to maximize your gains from our knowledge and expertise over time. And it can't happen if we're not on the same page, or if there's not some sort of personal connection underpinning the financial relationship. Beyond that, it won't bear fruit if we just seem to rub each other the wrong way. No advisor's technical knowledge is worth the trouble if it's not a good personal fit.

So, what is the "no jerks" rule? Well, to quote a common expression, "We both know it when we see it."

And lastly, what do I mean by we're not "yes men/women"? Simply put, we are not order takers. Our job is not just to affirm every decision you make and place every trade you instruct. We are not your old school stock "broker." We are your fiduciary financial planner. We will tell you when we disagree. We will show you the numbers and the context so you can make the decision that makes the most sense for your financial future.

Now that we've established who *shouldn't* work with my firm, let's address the real value a great advisor provides—and it's not what most people think. Because it turns out the biggest financial-planning challenge isn't acquiring knowledge; it's implementing what you know.

36

An Advisor's Job Is to Move You to Action

"Financial success is not a hard science. It's a soft skill, where how you behave is more important than what you know."
—Morgan Housel

Over the years, I have had a few calls with prospective clients (keep in mind, these are people who reached out and scheduled a call with us . . . not the other way around) who love everything we have to say on our initial call, realize they have some large gaps in their planning in need of solving, and yet can't pull the trigger to actually get started.

Then, six months go by and they reach out again—except this time they schedule their next meeting within two minutes and tell us they're ready to get started on that very first meeting. What changed?

- They probably realized that all the information in the world didn't matter if they didn't have someone in their corner who would get them to act.
- They probably looked up one day and realized that six months had gone by since they first committed to setting up a financial plan, and while they had done research, read books, and begun to feel more educated . . . nothing had changed for them.

I once had a Right Fit call with a potential client who started by saying she'd taken the last year to "learn" and "research" what was out there when it came to her finances. She told us she wasn't really looking to do anything yet—she just wanted to learn.

Normally, I would have used our call time to try to answer her questions as best I could and then wish her well, knowing she wasn't serious about improving her financial situation.

But this time, I couldn't help but ask if she felt like she was in a better financial spot than she had been a year earlier. I wanted to know if her financial decision-making and behavior had changed since she set out on her journey to get advice and expertise. Had she acted or improved upon anything? What tangible/real-world value had she received for all those hours she'd spent gathering information? She was so committed to "exploring," I don't think she grasped my point.

CHANCE I WILL SEE A BLIND SPOT

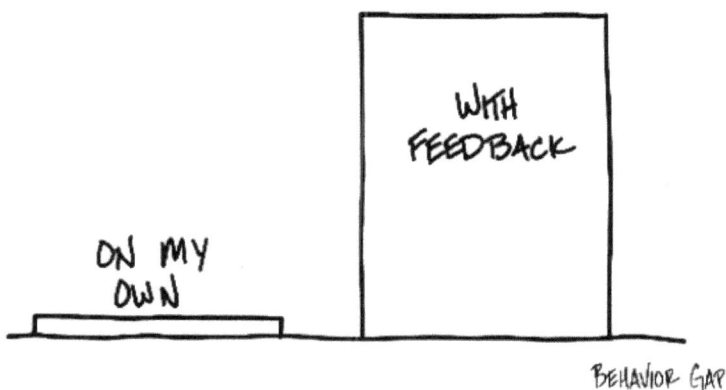

WITH
FEEDBACK

ON MY
OWN

BEHAVIOR GAP

My team's job is to help clients become aware of problems they didn't know they had and show them the solution. If the client does not take action (e.g., implement the 401[k] allocation change, complete the Roth conversion, re-title their brokerage account, change their beneficiary, or adjust their withholding), then we have not provided real value. Good ideas not implemented are just as useless as bad ideas.

This is how we measure ourselves: Did we inspire and/or educate the client enough for them to make the changes they need? This is not school. You do not get points for knowing what to do or understanding the mechanics. Your financial standing is only improved if you change your behavior or implement the tactical changes required to put you on a better financial footing.

My advisor team constantly keeps it top of mind that when it comes to building financial plans, we get paid to provide value, not volume. This means that:

- Having more pages in the client's financial plan doesn't mean we did a better job.
- Longer Zoom meetings with the client do not mean we did a better or even more comprehensive job.

No, as far as we're concerned, value is only measured by the action we inspire the client to take.

I would ask you to think about your own financial world with the same hyperfocus on outcomes. With so much information out there, it's easier than ever to get bogged down doing "research," reading how-to books, seeking out fifteen different advisors' thoughts, and getting educated. Has doing that ever moved anyone to take action, though? Is that really the best use of your time?

Here's the point: **It's not what you know, it's what you *actually get done* that matters.**

And understanding that implementation is the true value of financial planning leads us to an important warning: *Don't choose an advisor for the wrong reasons.* Believe it or not, the most common motivation for hiring a financial planner is actually the least important. In the next chapter, we'll take a look at what that motivation is and why it shouldn't matter.

37

The Worst Reason to Hire a Financial Planner

"I think the reason why we got into such idiocy in investment management is best illustrated by a story that I tell about the guy who sold fishing tackle. I asked him, 'My god, they're purple and green. Do fish really take these lures?' And he said, 'Mister, I don't sell to fish.'"

–Charlie Munger

I'm going to let you in on a little secret: A financial planner's job is not to beat the stock market, to be an expert stock picker, or to outperform an index.

A Certified Financial Planner (CFP®) is not a "money manager," "portfolio manager," or a "stock analyst" who spends his days building and structuring investment portfolios. That is literally a different job (and one that, as stated elsewhere, comes with diminishing returns).

A financial planner cannot predict the stock market better than anyone else out there. If you pick a financial planner because you think they will outperform the market, you will be sorely disappointed (at some point in the future!). They cannot predict which type of stocks will perform better over the next twelve months. We are privy to the same information as you are (which is the same that EVERYONE has access to—which is why our firm believes in low-cost, tax-efficient investing . . . but I digress!).

This is why I would be wary of a financial planner who answers the question "What is the average rate of return for your clients?" by actually providing historical performance numbers. I don't even know where to start with that. First, all clients have different risk capacities, preferences, and time horizons. They all started investing at different times and are adding/withdrawing money at different points. But putting all that aside, there's a bigger problem. Any portfolio returns you're looking at assume that the way the money is allocated now is the way the money was invested during that entire time . . . and that's hardly ever the case!

The actual outcomes will differ because the current version of the portfolio has the benefit of hindsight and has been updated over the years as new information emerged. Anybody can create a hypothetical portfolio that would have performed really well over the last ten years . . . the portfolio is allocated the way it does now because of what happened over the last ten years! Most likely, whatever portfolio you're looking at didn't achieve those "historical" returns because you likely would have owned different positions throughout that period, and the portfolio is only considering the model's allocation today.

This isn't anything nefarious—it's really the only way to analyze how a current portfolio model would have done in the past. Most folks who do this are genuinely trying to answer the client's question; I just believe they should, instead, be reframing the question. Projecting the *current* allocation backward is a truly useless exercise in evaluating an investment strategy for the future, and it can lead folks into thinking about investing in a counterproductive way.

As a simple example, let s say an advisor shows you a portfolio that has a 20% allocation to Nvidia . . . well, that portfolio's historical (read: hypothetical) returns are going to look amazing!! Except if the model only added such a large allocation to Nvidia six months ago (which you wouldn't know just by looking at the current portfolio), the ACTUAL returns of the investors who were in that model over the last five years would be wildly different than the returns you're looking at. It's rarely an apples-to-apples comparison.

So, what's a better way to answer that question? Whenever anyone asks me, here are the three things I emphasize:

1) To most directly answer the question, as best I can: As a firm, we believe markets are efficient, and that attempting to "beat" the market through active stock selection is a fool's errand. Instead, we strive to capture the entire market's return in a cost-effective and tax-efficient way. Given this, Mr. or Ms. Client, your "returns" with us will be similar to the performance of the asset classes we're investing in (large cap, small cap, international, etc.) as a whole. We will look to create additional value to your investments through tax optimization.

2) I think the real question you're asking is, "Will the cost of your services give my family a good return in terms of more wealth, time, and peace of mind?" This is a great question, and I always make sure to spend some time discussing it with the client.

3) Ultimately, it's almost impossible to gauge the future investment returns of a firm you're thinking about hiring. In truth, I think the best way to attempt to "measure" a wealth management firm's investment performance is to look at their investment philosophy (they should have one), their assets under

management, and their longevity. It's imperfect, but the reality is that if a firm you're considering working with has been around for five or ten years and has been growing its managed assets and head-count, well . . . they're probably doing a solid job stewarding their client's money. It's really hard to retain clients if you're performing terribly!

These three points, together, make sense to the plan-ning-oriented investment clients we want to work with.

If, however, achieving slightly higher investment returns on your quarterly statement is the *only* reason you're thinking about hiring a financial advisor, then honestly, you should consider going it alone—and I have told prospects as much when I get the sense that's really the only "service" they're looking for. A financial advisor's job is to utilize all the different areas of your family's finances (e.g., cash flow, investments, insurance, estate planning, tax optimization, and goal setting) to create more wealth for your family, while giving you back more of your time, energy, and attention.

After all, would you rather earn 8% in your managed portfolios and have $5M net worth in twenty years, or would you rather have earned 6.5% in your managed port-folios and have $7M of total wealth (through diligent cash flow management, tax optimization, RSU planning, plan-ning touch points, and so on)?

Close to 100% of people would pick the latter, because while investment success can be a means to greater wealth, it is not wealth itself. (This is not to say that you can only have one, or that they're in opposition . . . it's just to illustrate a point.)

I have had thousands of conversations with high-income professionals all around the country looking for guidance. I can immediately tell whether the person I'm speaking with truly understands what a financial planner's purpose is, and whether that person would benefit from professional guidance.

So, if beating the market isn't the reason to hire a financial planner, what are the real factors that would drive you toward that decision?

- You want a trusted partner to share in the decision-making process whenever you are contemplating a life decision, big or small, such as: buying or renting a new home, refinancing a housing project versus paying cash, private school versus public school, changing careers, going from two household incomes to one, paying down debt versus investing your bonus, taking a sabbatical from work, how best to help an elderly relative, moving from the city to the suburbs (or from one state to another), renting out your old home versus selling, or paying off your mortgage faster or slower.

- You realize that time is your most precious commodity (and the only one you can't make more of). This means that hiring a proactive and competent financial planner doesn't just improve your tactical decision-making;

it will also, by definition, contribute to an improved quality of life overall, by giving you back your time so you can do more of what you want to do.

- You no longer want to maintain the psychological burden of managing every aspect of your family's financial affairs by yourself. You want to get rid of that voice in the back of your head that wonders, "Am I missing anything? Will I have enough? Am I heading in the right direction?" You want a true partner who is being paid to shoulder that burden and who has the expertise and temperament to live with it every day, so you don't have to.

- You want an objective (outside) voice telling you the things you don't necessarily want to hear, and holding you accountable to get the stuff done that you've been absent-mindedly putting off for years. Like setting up a monthly investment strategy (and sticking to it), buying more life insurance because your family is growing, or setting up an estate plan with guardianships and trustees. There is a reason most people will do more push-ups if a trainer is standing next to them and counting them out loud than if they were working out at home by themselves.

- You don't have the time, energy, or inclination to manage your cash flow, investment strategy, insurance strategy, or the ever-changing tax environment, or to ascertain your overall financial health based on dozens of overlapping variables on a regular basis. (Just reading this sentence made your head spin, didn't it?!)

At the end of the day, you should hire a professional planner because the (financial, mental, day-to-day, emotional) value you receive from the relationship is greater by a multitude than the total price you are paying for it. For readers who nodded along to the points above and identified with any of them, well, a relationship with a great financial planner will simply prove to be invaluable.

Alternatively, maybe nothing on this list resonates with you. Maybe you're saying some variation of, "I kind of love doing this all myself. I love my spreadsheets, I don't mind spending my time doing all this," or, "Ehh, that all seems too intangible to me, it doesn't MOVE me to action." In that case, I'd say you probably aren't going to enjoy working with a comprehensive CFP® in an ongoing capacity (even if it would benefit you).

As we wrap this chapter up, let's get very clear and specific. Here are some ways a financial planner will provide tangible and immediate tactical value that goes beyond any "rate of return" on a statement:

- **Tax-efficient investing:** Placing tax-sensitive holdings in tax-deferred accounts and tax-affected holdings in taxable accounts.
- **Retirement tax planning**: Taking advantage of backdoor Roth IRAs and mega backdoor Roth IRAs, and

devising a strategy to convert IRA money to Roth IRA money to lower your tax liability.

- **Protection planning:** Ensuring that you have adequate disability/life/long-term care insurance to protect your financial foundation. Earning 8% in your portfolio doesn't mean anything if you get injured and your $500K annual salary gets replaced by a measly $2K per month because you didn't have enough coverage.

- **Account titling:** Setting up portfolios, either individually owned, jointly held, or TOD (Transfer-on-Death), depending on the circumstances. Having primary beneficiaries and contingent beneficiaries on ALL of your accounts (and updating all of them).

- **Withdrawal/distribution planning:** Helping you to withdraw money from your accounts in a way that makes the most sense for your taxes and asset allocation.

- **Education planning:** Creating an education planning program that straddles the sometimes contradictory goals of tax efficiency and flexibility.

- **Cash flow investing:** Helping to build a system that will prioritize where your money should be going each month, such as 401(k)s, 529 plans, taxable investments, Roth IRAs, insurance, savings accounts, stocks, I bonds, treasuries, and so on.

All these decisions play a significant role in helping you get closer to hitting your net worth targets and achieving your financial goals. And none of them are reflected in a particular portfolio's "rate of return."

So far, we've beaten you over the head (in a pleasant way?!) with the areas of planning that should be relevant to a mid-career professional. Given all the areas we can help with, it's worth discussing why some people wait so long to get started. Why do some people never get around to planning for their financial future (whether on their own or with a professional partner)? Sometimes it comes down to cost, which most people don't like to admit. Many qualified prospects hesitate at the doorway and never step through because they can't get around the fees. So, that's where we turn next!

38

When Hiring a Planner: Price Is What You Pay, Value Is What You Get

"Money's greatest intrinsic value—and this can't be overstated—is its ability to give you control over your time."
–Morgan Housel

I love taking the Right Fit calls I've mentioned throughout this book. These are a critical first step for both Drucker Wealth and our prospective client, as the call sets the stage for what working together could mean. During these fifteen- to twenty-minute calls, I get a better understanding of their financial situation, what they believe they need help with, what they're motivated to do about it, and where they're ultimately trying to go. We figure out together whether my team is the right fit to help them bridge the gap between their financial present and their financial future by providing them with real financial planning.

This call is introductory in nature. Sometimes, I share a few ideas with them before letting them know we may not be the right firm (if I don't think their situation warrants our level of service or associated fees) or that there are a few more basic strategies they should think about before we engage.

If, however, I do think we can deliver meaningful value and that we'd be a good fit, I will set up the next call: a financial discovery meeting. This next conversation is a forty-five to sixty-minute Zoom meeting with one of our lead advisors, where we will do a deeper dive into the client's financial priorities and determine whether we're all 100% comfortable (and excited) to begin working together.

There's one story I still remember, because it's one of the only times I've ever been speechless on a Right Fit call. A few years ago, a prospective client told me, by way of explaining her decision not to move forward with our firm, "I love your approach and your process, and I absolutely know I need a plan, but I just don't feel like I should spend money on this right now."

On her Right Fit call, she had acknowledged that she:

- Spends too much money
- Needed help organizing her cash flow
- Wanted to better understand whether she was veering off course from accomplishing her financial goals

To reiterate, she freely admitted that she was frivolous with her income and spent too much money . . . yet she chose to draw the line at spending money on a financial planning partnership that would address and solve those same financial worries. As they say, you can bring a horse to water, but you can't make them drink.

I found it a valuable conversation. There's a difference between *hoping* you will become financially independent and *doing* what it takes to get there.

If I may be so bold, she chose to focus on the short-term cost of our guidance over the long-term value (both in tangible dollars and in peace of mind) that such a plan is designed to provide over the next twenty to thirty years. I'd wager to say that she probably spent more on her credit card the following month than our total cost would have been to analyze, break down, and evaluate her past, present, and future financial standing.

In short, she made the decision about planning her financial future the same way I determine what pair of pants I might buy. (Cue my internal dialogue: "Well, they all keep my legs warm, so lowest price tag wins.")

This story sticks out because, truthfully, I can't remember the last client who didn't move forward because of our fees. For one thing, our prospective clients are aware of the fees from our website and have already internalized them by the time they reach out. I also think that as folks get older and busier and their lives get more complicated, they start to safeguard their time more diligently and respect professional advice more fully. Regardless, as not everyone who reads this book is going to have OUR exact client profile, it felt important to include this chapter anyway!

When it comes to financial advice, you can have it cheap, fast, or great. But you can only pick two! In my experience of working with outside professionals (like coaches, consultants, and our business CPA, among others), I've come to realize that cost is only a factor in the absence of value.

In those relationships where I'm the client, if I feel I'm getting the value that I want, then I am more than happy to pay these professionals their keep. They are doing work I can't or don't want to do, and they are going above and beyond to take care of me. That's enough for me. So, when I am in the advisor seat, I am proud to share with prospective and current clients that we are never trying to be the lowest-cost option available. I always think of the joke about flying: "It's better not to think about the fact that every part of the plane you're sitting in was built by the lowest-cost provider." Our goal is not to provide the lowest cost. It's to provide unparalleled value.

With something as serious and life-altering as financial decision-making, your choice should hinge on the value you expect to receive relative to the price you will be paying. Price by itself is not a barometer of anything.

Ultimately, what I'm asking you to reckon with is this: What are you willing to spend and do to create the financial future you deserve?

Now, if you've decided that you *are* ready to get professional help, how do you make that decision? What should you be looking for in an advisor?

39

Financial Advisor Models: The Value of Independent Fiduciary Advice

"Show me the incentive, and I'll show you the outcome."
–Charlie Munger

There are wonderful financial planners working in every type of advisory model and at every type of advisory firm. I know great advisors everywhere: big banks, insurance companies, broker-dealers, and independent firms.

The problem is that certain structures also make it easier for bad advisors (and financial salespeople) to sneak through the doors. And when it's really hard to pick out the good advisors from the bad (and I don't envy you, it is!), you're better off just avoiding the firms where the incentive structures make it harder to be a great advisor and easier for bad apples to sneak through.

I'll put it like this: If I wasn't a financial planner and my sister asked me who she should work with, I would tell her to start by looking for a CFP® Professional, working at an independent fiduciary RIA (Registered Investment Advisor), who specializes in working with clients like her (she's married with three kids, early thirties, etc.). Then, after she had cleared those hurdles, it would be a matter of personal comfort, trust, and fit.

Let's break these down one-by-one.

Being a CFP® doesn't mean you're a great advisor . . . of course. But someone being a CFP® does tell me that they are probably committed to this as a career (because passing the exams and the experience requirements takes time) and it shows some level of applied knowledge, learning, and focus. Simply put, you shouldn't pick an advisor because they are a CFP®, but I, personally, would rule out an advisor who isn't.

I would tell my sister to choose an RIA because Independent RIAs are fiduciaries who are required to put their clients' interests ahead of their own, and they get paid only by the clients they serve, through the advisory fees they charge (rather than commissions). Registered Investment Advisors can also utilize any number of third-party custodians to hold and safeguard client assets. Common custodians include Schwab, Fidelity, Pershing, Altruist, and LPL. Because client accounts are held at a third-party custodian, when working with an Independent RIA, your money is still being handled by some of the largest and most secure institutions in the world. The difference is that RIA firms, unlike some of these other models, don't work for these institutions, are not paid by these institutions, and can pick up their ball and go to a different court anytime they want.

Similarly, RIAs, unlike most of the other models, can utilize any investment portfolios, strategies, or funds that they like when advising their clients! (I don't want to speak for any other RIA, but at Drucker Wealth, we are fund agnostic: It makes zero difference to us, in terms of our pay, which fund family we utilize, so we typically use funds from Vanguard and Dimensional as they have a proven track record and low costs.)

Explained another way, as an RIA firm, there is no corporate "mother ship" (like a bank or an insurance company) telling us how to invest or which funds to use or incentivizing the sale of their own mutual funds or insurance products.

Lastly, because RIAs are owned by firm partners* (who are usually advisors at the firm) rather than a corporate behemoth, we are independent to utilize the investment funds, technology partners, operation systems, and service models we think work BEST for OUR clients. All of this is to say that RIAs are structured and incentivized the same way as most other professional service businesses (like law firms, accounting firms, and consulting firms), while the rest of the industry is NOT.

It really is that simple. When you're working with an advisor at a big box shop, there can be sales quotas, proprietary funds that you get compensated more for using, and less of a focus on fiduciary and holistic advice, because that's not always what the advisors are being paid to provide.

Again, this does NOT mean all advisors at RIAs are great (they're not!) or that most advisors at the big box shops are bad (not at all!)—it's just that our incentives and fee structure are more directly aligned with yours, and we have *fewer* conflicts of interest. (Despite what they might say, nobody in business can entirely avoid conflicts of interest, but working with fiduciary and independent firms does MINIMIZE them drastically!)

---

* Some RIAs are owned wholly or in part by private equity firms. That's not my cup of tea and is not something I can ever imagine Drucker Wealth doing . . . but these firms are, in my opinion, still on average, MUCH better than the non-RIA alternatives.

Speaking of fiduciary and holistic advice, one of the most common things I hear from people who are curious about working with us is: "Well, financial advisor John Smith at XYZ Big Corporate Firm manages a few of my accounts . . . but . . . I'm reaching out because I feel like his team doesn't 'do' financial planning. We have an annual check-in call, but it's only ever about the investment accounts themselves . . . I still don't feel like I have an actual plan, and that's what I'm looking for."

I always try to dance around the question that immediately comes to my mind: "Well, if they don't do financial planning, what is it they're doing for you?" It's at this point that these people realize they may not actually have a financial planner. They have an investment professional who charges commission for financial products or a fee for assets under management, but without any awareness or insight into their broader financial life.

If your advisor spends their day tracking the markets, hosts webinars on whether this is the year for emerging markets, and only ever talks to you about your investment portfolios, they are not doing real financial planning.

If your advisor spends their day talking to you about your cash flow, how much you are saving for your kids' college versus how much you need for retirement, and how your long-term planning will provide opportunities within your 401(k) allocation . . . they are doing real financial planning.

Any investment professional can tell you if your accounts are doing well.

A financial planner can tell if your goals, your cash flow, your investments, and your tax planning are coordinated, and whether you're on the right track for your financial future.

Regardless of what I've shared in this book, only *you* can make the decision about whether you ultimately want to hire a financial advisor or not. What I hope I've conveyed in this final section is that if you do decide to seek professional help, it's vital to make sure you're not paying for someone simply to manage your investments. It is NOT worth paying a premium fee for investment advice alone. If you have an "advisor" who just manages your investments, you are probably overpaying them. Financial planning is about tax optimization, cash flow management, estate planning, risk management, life planning, retirement planning, employee benefits, education funding, housing analysis, family planning, and insurance. If you have an advisor who covers all of that, you might be underpaying them relative to the value they provide.

If You Have Two Advisors, You Don't Even Have One!

In football, a longstanding truism is that if you have two quarterbacks, you don't really even have one. What does this mean? Well, put simply . . . if it's not *obvious* who your starting quarterback should be, it means you really don't have one who is truly good enough to lead your team. That means you're in a rough spot!

Put another way: If your quarterback isn't good enough to be a *clear* starter on your team, he's definitely not going to be good enough to beat another team! How is this relevant to your quest for financial independence? I recently had a client who was close to completing his Financial Life Plan® with us.

Up to this point, here is what his financial world consisted of:

- A few rollover IRAs with one firm
- A few investment accounts with another firm
- A few investment accounts with a third firm

As part of the financial plan, we completed our comprehensive analysis of all his investments (including performance, cost, asset allocation, and risk tolerance) and walked him through all his accounts and how they fit together. Broadly speaking, he was in great shape. Yes, there were changes to be made and more efficient ways of managing things, but that wasn't my issue. My most definitive recommendation was to say, "I hope you decide to continue working with us, but no matter what, you need to pick ONLY ONE firm to manage your investments and oversee your planning!"

"Why?" he asked.

My straightforward reply was this: "There is absolutely no reason to be paying advisor fees for three different investment strategies, when not one of them has any idea what the other is doing. Not one of them is acting as your fiduciary advisor and overseeing your financial life! They're all just managing the pot of money you've placed with them . . . nothing else. Even if they wanted to do more, they wouldn't be able to with the way you've set things up!"

I went on: "If you have three different financial advisors with three different investment approaches, in actuality, you don't really have any—and you're more disorganized than if you did this yourself!"

A financial advisor should not be paid only to manage your investments. They should be helping to coordinate your entire financial life. Pick one advisor who's up for the job, and whom you trust and like, and then . . . let them help you!

PART 5
CONCLUSION

"The secret to getting ahead is getting started."
–Mark Twain

40

What Are You Waiting For?

"Procrastination is the most common manifestation of resistance because it's the easiest to rationalize. We don't tell ourselves, 'I'm never going to write my symphony.' Instead we say, 'I am going to write my symphony; I'm just going to do it tomorrow.'"
— Steven Pressfield, *The War of Art*

At the beginning of this book—if you can remember back that far!—I told you that I start every day with hot coffee, lemon water, and a run along the East River.

I confessed that during that run I usually listen to podcasts, but sometimes I'll start thinking about my clients instead. It might be someone new, like Marc and Laura, whom you met in that introductory chapter. It might be someone I've worked with for years. And it might be the clients I'm excited to meet, people I hope to help in the future.

Including you.

In this book, I've shared dozens of stories about working with clients, each with their own unique challenges and opportunities. I've worked with some great people over the years. And though their individual circumstances may differ, at the heart of every story is a hard-working, high-achieving professional trying to make wise financial decisions for themselves and their families.

Perhaps you see yourself in their struggle. The impressive income. The busy career. The growing family demands. The finances scattered in a dozen different directions.

Maybe, as you prepare to finish reading and go on with your life, you're even thinking, *Whoa. That was a lot.*

And yeah. It *was* a lot! But I hope this book doesn't become yet another title on your Kindle, something you read once and never look at again. We've all got those.

But this is different. This is a playbook for your financial future—and by reading it, you've taken the first crucial step. Now you know the big secret: Earning well doesn't automatically translate to building wealth. That's huge.

So, what now?

First, take a breath. Financial independence isn't achieved overnight. The fact that you've finished this book puts you ahead of 90% of your peers . . . high five!

Before we say goodbye, I want you to ask yourself three questions.

1. **"What financial myths have I been holding onto that this book has forced me to rethink?"**

2. **"What has to happen in the next twenty years for me to consider myself financially successful?"**

3. **"Which financial issue do I need clarity on within the next two months because it's keeping me up at night?"** (Or to be less dramatic—because it annoys me every two weeks when I think about it randomly while I'm driving the kids to school.)

The myths are your biggest blind spots, the so-called truths that have been whispering pernicious lies in your ear for years, or even decades. Which ones have been holding you back? Be honest. We've all fallen for at least a few. Did you think your home was your best investment without really checking the numbers? (As you now know, it's way more complex than that.) Were you chasing tax deductions without a lifetime tax strategy? Have you been letting temporary market declines drive permanent investment decisions?

Your answers to questions two and three are even more exciting. Number two reveals your priorities—the destination(s) you're navigating your life toward—and number three paves the way for your first action step. That's powerful.

You don't have to do everything at once. In fact, I don't recommend it! That's like trying to eat an entire cheesecake in one bite. Delicious in theory. Disastrous in practice.

I'll tell you something else they don't teach you in school: Building wealth is as much an emotional journey as a financial one. You'll experience doubt. Markets will crash (they always do). You'll question your plan. You'll be tempted by whatever investing fad your neighbor won't shut up about and the exciting tax strategy that somehow found its way into your Instagram algorithm. You'll worry you're not doing enough. Or that you're not doing it quickly enough.

This is normal. I'd worry if you *didn't* feel like this from time to time.

When doubts creep in, return to your priorities. Remember why you started. Was it for your kids? For freedom from financial stress? For options later in life when you're retired and sailing around the world, watching the stamps in your passport stack up?

Whatever your "why," keep it front and center. Write it down. Stick it on your refrigerator next to your kid's artwork. It won't be nearly as cute, but it's just as important.

After that, it's all about bringing the "how" to fruition. My hope for you is that you find a financial partner to help you implement the strategies you've learned about in this book.

Professional guidance has tremendous value. Think of it like fitness. Could you work out alone? Sure. Would you be as consistent without a trainer counting your reps, correcting your form, and pushing you through that last set when your arms feel like noodles? Probably not. Does doing it alone make you more prone to injury and setbacks? Absolutely.

I've never met a client who regretted getting their financial house in order. I've met plenty, though, who regretted waiting so long to start.

Don't wait until work slows down—because it never does. Don't wait until after your next promotion. Don't wait until the kids are older.

Start today. With one step. Then do the next right thing. And the next.

Small changes, consistently applied, create massive results over time. I've seen the relief on clients' faces when they finally understand where they stand financially. I've witnessed their excitement when they realize they can achieve goals they thought were unreachable. I've celebrated with them as they've transformed their relationship with money.

That's how you move from being a HENRY to being truly wealthy—not just in dollars, but in options, freedom, and peace of mind.

That journey is available to you. The roadmap is clear. The tools are in your hands.

Now go make it happen!

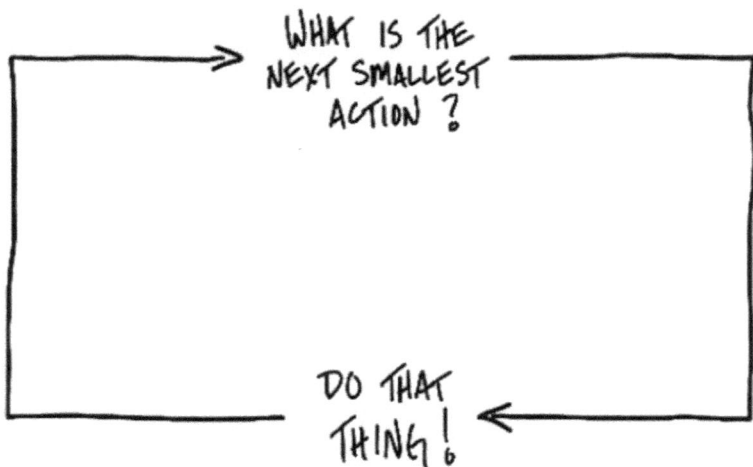

WHAT IS THE NEXT SMALLEST ACTION?

DO THAT THING!

Let's Keep the
Conversation Going

You've taken the time to read this book, reflect on your financial life, and start thinking about the future you want to build. That's no small step. But reading is only the beginning. The real transformation happens when you put these ideas into practice.

If you're ready to:

- Finally feel confident about your financial plan
- Align your wealth with your family's biggest priorities
- Create a roadmap for the next property, the next stage of your career, and the next chapter of your life . . .

. . . I'd love to help guide you there.

My team and I at Drucker Wealth specialize in working with mid-career professionals and families earning $300K+ who are ready to go from "doing well" to living with true financial flexibility (and on the path toward financial freedom). We will build a customized, actionable strategy to build your wealth, fund your dreams, and finally answer your/your family's question: "Are we going to be okay?"

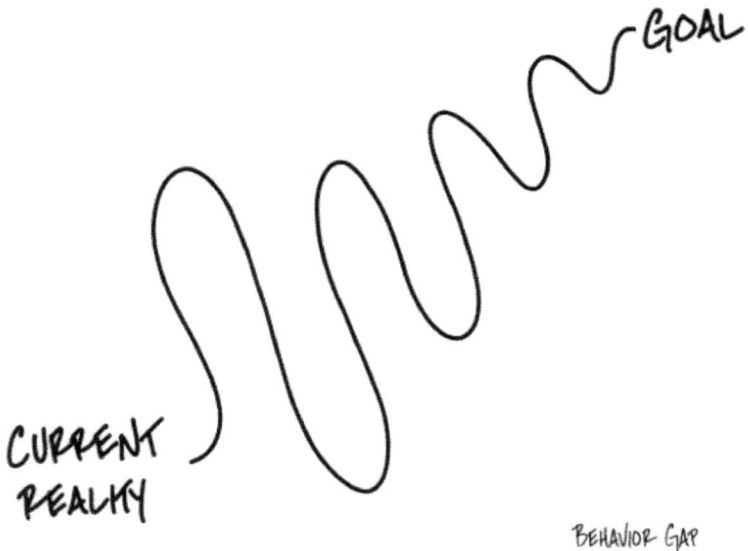

GOAL

CURRENT REALITY

BEHAVIOR GAP

Visit DruckerWealth.com to learn more about our Financial Life Plan® program, schedule your Right Fit call, or just to explore more resources.
- Schedule a Right Fit call: calendly.com/gideon-6/15min
- Resources: druckerwealth.com/book

You can also connect with me directly on:

- LinkedIn: linkedin.com/in/gideondrucker
- Instagram: @druckerwealth

Your income is already powerful. Together, we'll make sure it becomes life-changing.

Giving Back

One of my biggest motivations for building wealth is being able to use my money to make an impact on the causes that inspire me and the people I am committed to supporting.

With that in mind, I wanted to share a bit about the two causes to which I will be donating 100% of the book's proceeds:

The Travis Manion Foundation
travismanion.org
The UJA's Federation: Israel At War
ujafedny.org/israel-at-war

Travis Manion Foundation

This charity is named after Marine Corps 1st Lt. Travis Manion, who gave the ultimate sacrifice on April 29, 2007, on his second deployment to Iraq. While on patrol searching for a suspected insurgent house in Fallujah, Travis, his fellow Marines, and Iraqi Army counterparts were ambushed. Travis led a counterattack against enemy forces, drawing fire away from his wounded comrades and allowing every member of his patrol to survive. Travis won the Silver Star and Bronze Star with Valor for his actions under attack. He died a hero.

The foundation's mission is to empower veterans and the families of fallen heroes to inspire and develop character in future generations. With our support, veterans continue their service, build connections with each other, and thrive in their post-military lives through mentoring programs, service-based trips, and community service projects. As a result, communities prosper, and the character of our nation's heroes lives on in the next generation.

The ethos of the Travis Manion Foundation is "If not me, then who?" It's an attitude and a way of approaching life we should all strive for.

UJA Federation: Israel At War

On October 7, 2023, Israel was savagely invaded and attacked by Hamas terrorists. Over 1,200 innocent Israeli citizens were brutally murdered, thousands more injured, and over 240 Israelis were kidnapped—including babies, the elderly, and entire families—before being dragged into the Hamas dungeons. Entire communities in Southern Israel were devastated. It was the single deadliest day for the Jewish people since the Holocaust.

In the two years that followed, over 500 Israeli soldiers lost their lives fighting in Israel's defensive war aimed at uprooting the Hamas terrorists and returning the hostages. Hundreds of thousands more Israeli civilians were uprooted from their homes (in Northern Israel) because of Hezbollah rocket fire.

As a former paratrooper in the Israel Defense Forces, my heart mourns for my brothers and sisters in Israel, including the families of two of my officers who were killed defending our people.

Two years on—the UJA continues to provide essential support to the victims of October 7 as they rebuild their lives following this horrific attack.

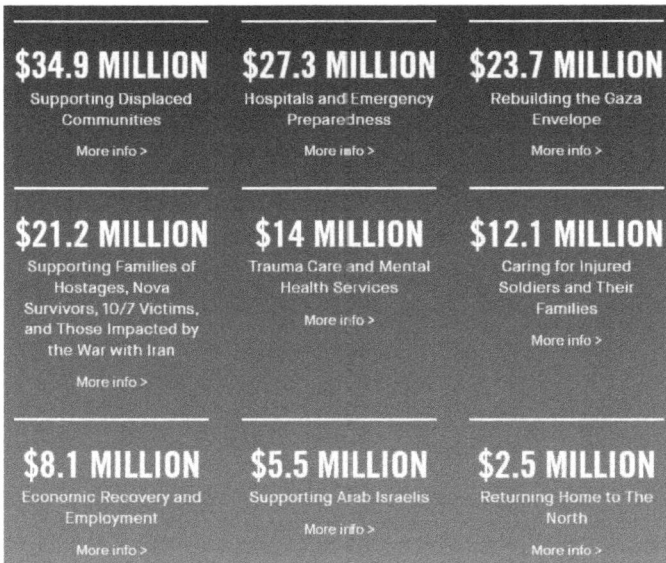

$34.9 MILLION	$27.3 MILLION	$23.7 MILLION
Supporting Displaced Communities	Hospitals and Emergency Preparedness	Rebuilding the Gaza Envelope
More info >	More info >	More info >
$21.2 MILLION	$14 MILLION	$12.1 MILLION
Supporting Families of Hostages, Nova Survivors, 10/7 Victims, and Those Impacted by the War with Iran	Trauma Care and Mental Health Services	Caring for Injured Soldiers and Their Families
More info >	More info >	More info >
$8.1 MILLION	$5.5 MILLION	$2.5 MILLION
Economic Recovery and Employment	Supporting Arab Israelis	Returning Home to The North
More info >	More info >	More info >

Endnotes

Chapter 8: Personal Finance Is More Personal Than It Is Finance

1. Tim Maurer, CFP® finance motto, https://tim.signaturefd.com.

Chapter 11: The Eleven Most Impactful Financial Myths

2. Ben Carlson, "Historical Returns for Stocks, Bonds & Cash," A Wealth of Common Sense, January 14, 2024, https://awealthofcommon-sense.com/2024/01/historical-returns-for-stocks-bonds-cash/.

3. Ashby Daniels, "It's Official", January newsletter. Further source: https://yardeni.com/our-charts.

Chapter 12: Investing: Volatility is NOT Risk

4. Arielle O'Shea and James Royal, "The Average Stock Market Return: About 10%," NerdWallet, September 25, 2025, https://www.nerdwallet.com/article/investing/average-stock-market-return.

5. Per FactSet, Standard & Poor's, Yardeni Research, and NYU Stern School.

6. "S&P 500 Earnings—90 Year Historical Chart," MacroTrends, https://www.macrotrends.net/1324/s-p-500-earnings-history.

7. Nick Murray, "Fifty Years Ago: The Day the Great Postwar Bull Market Died," LT Wealth, January 12, 2023, https://ltwealth.ca/the-day-the-great-postwar-bull-market-died.

8. Per Morningstar Chart, Ibbotson SBBI (stocks, bonds, bills, and inflation).

9. Per JP Morgan Asset Management, Robert Shiller, Strategas/Ibbotson.

10. Clearnomics, Standard & Poor's, Federal Reserve and stock chart: https://yardeni.com/our-charts.

11. Standard & Poor's and Clearnomics.

12. Murray, "Fifty Years Ago."

13. Jeremy Siegel, *Stocks for the Long Run*, 6th Edition (New York: McGraw Hill, 2022).

14. Carlson, "Historical Returns for Stocks, Bonds & Cash."

Chapter 14: Investing: Why I Don't Pick Individual Stocks

15. Bessembinder, Hendrik (Hank), *Which U.S. Stocks Generated the Highest Long-Term Returns?* (November 11, 2024). Available at SSRN: https://ssrn.com/abstract=4897069 or http://dx.doi.org/10.2139/ssrn.4897069.

16. Brinson, Hood, and Beebower Study (1986).

17. MSCI World Index historical performance.

18. Bessembinder, "Do Stocks Outperform Treasury Bills?" Journal of Financial Economics, 2018.

Chapter 15: Investing: Inflation Is the Silent Killer

19. According to SPIVA (S&P Indices Versus Active) Scorecards.

20. J.P. Morgan Asset Management, *Guide to Retirement 2025*, https://am.jpmorgan.com/us/en/asset-management/adv/insights/retirement-insights/guide-to-retirement/.

21. Mark Riepe, "Longevity Risk: Could You Outlive Your Savings?," Schwab Brokerage, August 28, 2025, https://www.schwab.com/learn/story/longevity-risk-could-you-outlive-your-savings.

Chapter 16: Investing: What Do Declining Stock Prices Mean for You?

22. Cory Mitchell, "Historical Average Stock Market Returns for S&P 500 (5-Year to 150-Year Averages)," Trade That Swing, September 15, 2025, https://tradethatswing.com/average-historical-stock-market-returns-for-sp-500-5-year-up-to-150-year-averages/.

Chapter 17: Investing: Diversification and Asset Allocation

23. From December 31, 2000, to December 31, 2010, the MSCI ACWI ex USA Index had a total return of 71.53% compared to 15.07% for the S&P 500 Index.

Chapter 19: Home Ownership: Our (Primary) Home-Buying Philosophy

24. Sean Ross, "Has Real Estate or the Stock Market Performed Better Historically?," Investopedia, December 2, 2024, https://www.investopedia.com/ask/answers/052015/which-has-performed-better-historically-stock-market-or-real-estate.asp.

25. Jaclene Begley and Mark Palim, "What Are the Biggest Costs of Home-ownership? (Hint: It's Not What You Might Think)," Fannie Mae I Perspectives Blog, March 9, 2022, https://www.fanniemae.com/research-and-insights/perspectives/biggest-costs-homeownership.

Chapter 21: Real Estate Investing: The Allure vs. the Reality

26. Morgan Housel, *The Psychology of Money* (Harriman House, 2020), 45.

Chapter 26: Tax Loss Harvesting

27. Chart Source: FactSet. The Russell 3000 Index is an unmanaged index considered representative of the US stock market.

Chapter 33: Intro to Restricted Stock Units

28. Per IRS Notice 2007-49, the value of vested RSUs is treated as ordinary income, calculated as the number of shares vested multiplied by the fair market value on the vesting date.